A LIFE OF TRIUMPH

IRH PRESS

A LIFE of TRIUMPH

Unleashing Your Light Upon the World

RYUHO OKAWA

IRH PRESS
New York

Library of Congress Cataloging-in-Publication Data

ISBN 13: 978-1-942125-11-2
ISBN 10: 1-942125-11-9

Printed in China

First Edition
Second printing

Book Design: Jess Morphew
Cover image © Shutterstock / grop
Interior images; Clouds © Shutterstock / Sundra,
Mountain © Shutterstock / grop

CONTENTS

CHAPTER FOUR
Creating Your Own Destiny | 121

CHAPTER FIVE

Discovering New Horizons of Success | 199

PUBLISHER'S NOTE

A Life of Triumph, by Ryuho Okawa, was published with the simple desire to inspire us with hope, courage, and a never-ceasing flow of energy when we need to find confidence in our power to rise above our struggles and pave the way forward to our dreams. There are poems and discussions that cover a range of themes, such as on having hopes and dreams for our future, summoning our courage and love for others, resolutely believing that we are children of God, and having strong faith in our inner light to spread God's light throughout the world.

All of the ideas presented in this book are based on the firm conviction that when we live with a positive, spiritual perspective on life, we can never truly be defeated by any problem or adversity that may befall us, nor can our happiness ever be destroyed by any event or circumstance that may arise in our journey through this world. This is because this perspective gives us the confidence that we are here in this world to fulfill a meaningful purpose—one that is even larger than just the scope of this life and that is designed to bring an abiding, lasting happiness to our eternal soul.

Ryuho Okawa presents a philosophy of life that closely resembles the teachings espoused by the philosophy of New Thought, especially as this philosophy has been articulated in Japan, and for a good reason: a large part of this book was inspired by the divine guidance of the Shinto god Ameno Minakanushi, who is one of the central gods of the Shinto religion. He is often considered to be the source of the universe, a creator-like god, but in truth, he was a god of Japan who lived in the flesh approximately three thousand years ago and became one of the central figures that laid the foundations of the Japanese civilization in the region of southern Kyushu. He was an exceptional religious leader as well as a statesman, and he pioneered a government of the people by a leader who can hear and understand the words of the divinities. His foresight was so powerful and mystical and his discernment of human character so keen that everything he forecasted came true and all the statesmen he chose were virtuous. He earned great respect and the trust of his people.

Ameno Minakanushi believed so strongly and declared so persistently that goodness and light are the only Truths that his words inspired the realization of a world of happiness and light throughout his land. You will notice that the words in the pages that follow impart the same resolute belief in the essential goodness within human beings and the same staunch determination to actualize light in this world. Living with his philosophy is sure to inspire us to take action to realize a world of happiness and light as we face difficulties and issues around the globe that may otherwise discourage us and make us lose hope.

In this book, Ryuho Okawa introduces a philosophy that our effort to enhance beauty and strength in ourselves and others is as essential to our happiness as reflecting and improving on our flaws and weaknesses is. When we pay too much attention to our flaws, we humans are prone to developing a pessimistic outlook on life and, as a result, pushing happiness further away from our reach. If we aim instead to achieve dreams of higher value and to live with a broader perspective on life, what becomes vital to our achievements is looking on the bright side of all things. This mindset of thinking positively and constructively is essential to our ability to seize those evanescent opportunities of advancement when they momentarily appear before us.

This book shows that our desire for advancement arises not just for our own sake, but even more so for the sake of the world. The ability to contribute work of value to the world requires positivity, action, and optimism. To accomplish things of benefit to society, we need to begin by bringing ever-flowing light and hope to our own mind. Doing so is precious, in and of itself, and is also compassionate because it brings light and hope to those around us. The pages that follow will inspire an abiding, unfaltering belief in our inner light and awaken our power and our sense of true purpose of spreading God's light and realizing societies of happiness and prosperity in this world.

PREFACE

As I reviewed the manuscript of this book, I was amazed by the hope, courage, and energy that came welling forth within me. It is a marvel to me, indeed, that even I, the author, find my own spirits uplifted when I publish a book on a theme from New Thought. I am certain that you and all the readers around the world who pick up and read it will equally feel your spirits raised as much as a hundred times their previous level.

It is my hope that, in times of exhaustion, you will go through this book once more, and that in times of setback and despair, you will keep it always close at hand. I am certain that this book will be your promise of absolute triumph in this life.

Ryuho Okawa

FOUNDER AND CEO
Happy Science Group

Chapter One

BECOMING
A LIGHT
of
HAPPINESS

THE FOUR
PRINCIPLES
OF HAPPINESS

When you encounter joy in your life, do you feel a deeper sense of happiness by keeping the joy to yourself or by sharing the joy with those around you? You are probably more deeply happy when there are others, such as family members, to savor the joy with you.

This is because it is our essence, as human beings, to feel delight in seeing ourselves and others grow together in harmony. We decided to be born into this world out of our desire to help those who have never savored joy in life to find their own way forward to happiness. We left the world above of bliss and peace to come to this world, where there is suffering, because we hold the wish to create ideal societies of happiness for all. This was God's purpose in allowing humans to live among each other to form communities.

The creation of a truly utopian society like this depends, I believe, on our belief in the possibilities that we can achieve through growth and progress. What does progress mean? In essence, progress is the pursuit of the advancement of all of creation from this point where we are standing today. It is the growth of every person's state of mind and the development of the societies we live in. And God instilled a mission within the hearts of all humankind to resolve any discord that arises out of everyone's pursuit of their own self-growth and evolution so we can continue forward in harmony with one another.

This pursuit of progress in our own happiness as well as that of others is what I call *the principle of progress*. This is one of four principles in my chief philosophy, The Principles of Happiness, which enables us humans to find the right mindset that will allow us to truly grasp happiness in life.

The first principle is the principle of love. This idea was developed based on our human nature to feel happiness when our love for others arises purely from our heart's desire to give. It is the belief that true love is to give of our love for the sake of others and, furthermore, that happiness comes to those who give, while acts that take love will only keep happiness out of our reach.

The second principle is the principle of wisdom. This concept says that by cultivating a deep understanding of the Truths as humans we raise our enlightenment to a higher plane and enhance our ability to resolve all kinds of problems we run into, however varied they may be. Cultivating a deep and broad comprehension of the Truths as they apply to all matters of life is another essential way to happiness.

The third principle is the principle of self-reflection. This idea is closely related to the practice of continuously searching for the right mindset—what we call the Exploration of Right Mind. I believe that our heart and mind directly influence how happy we are. The sole thing that guarantees our happiness is the degree to which we have restored our mind to its original, authentic state.

What is the mind's original state? What is the authentic mind? First, I say with absolute certainty that, of all the billions of people on this globe, every one of us came from heaven. By the laws of the universe, no one is capable of being born from the world of hell. Imagine what would happen to the world of hell if this were allowed. Everyone would be born into this world to try to escape from the pain. Hell would then eventually be emptied and suddenly vanish.

So the fact that hell still exists means that no one is capable of being born from that world. By the laws of the universe, all those who are presently in hell need to, first, reach a certain degree of spiritual maturity so that they may be reinstated into heaven. Then, from there, they will have the chance to be reborn into this world.

There are large differences in the degrees of spiritual maturity that are found throughout heaven, but what all those in heaven have in common is a mind of complete peace and harmony. This is the original mind that we all once possessed.

But over the course of life in this world, our mind has become habituated to the coarser spiritual energies of this world, and so as we carried on our experiences on earth through various circumstances and environments, we gradually lost sight of our authentic mind. The surface of our mind became overcast with a layer of cloud, or a layer of rust.

Self-reflection is the practice of removing this rust and cloud from the mind. Without this practice, the cloud cannot be removed and we will be unable to restore our mind to its original state. Moreover, without our return to the authentic mind, we won't be able to live with complete peace, which is essential to living with hope in a bright future and a resolute sense of self-responsibility.

What, then, happens when we continue to form clouds

in our mind? As I mentioned earlier, there is a world of disharmony in the other world, called hell, which is full of beings who wish to escape from their pain. They accomplish this by living in apposition to people in this world with closely matching energies. This is the phenomenon of a negative influence by spiritual possession. Sadly, many people are living with these negative influences and with this state of mind completely unknowingly. This is a truly regrettable condition of the people of this world.

There are some people who are prone to believing that the spirits who are influencing us through spiritual possession are at fault for our unhappiness. But the truth is that something lying within our own mind is attracting them directly to us.

The world of thought and energy is based on the law that similar energies attract one another. Therefore, those who are being influenced and those who are doing the influencing both have the same state of mind. So it also follows that harmonizing the mind into peace will remove the part that is attracting the negative influence, as if to sever the ropes that have been attaching the two together. This will make the possession disappear.

We human beings were granted the power of free will, and with freedom comes responsibility for the way we choose to think, act, and make judgments. Because of free will, we are able to take responsibility for the outcomes of the decisions we make through life.

So what would become of us if, when we make a mistake as a result of the influence of another being, we tried to escape from our responsibility? What would happen to our independence as an individual? If we allowed this to go on, we would be succumbing to the complete mercy of another being. Thus, unless we live with a sense of responsibility for our own life, true happiness will remain far from our reach.

That is why I encourage everyone to keep their heart and mind polished and as free of rust and worldly vibrations as possible—so that you can keep a far distance between yourself and those of the other world in hell. This can be best achieved through the practice of self-reflection, such as by following the Eightfold Path, for example.

The fourth principle is the principle of progress. This principle is based on the belief that we humans are born and reborn hundreds and thousands of times with one purpose, which is to teach humanity about true happiness as we create ideal societies throughout the world.

BECOMING A WELLSPRING OF HAPPINESS

Achieving progress brings a true sense of happiness to us all. This is because it is our nature, as human beings, to wish to achieve good work that grows us into better people who can bring others happiness. We feel a sense of delight when our work creates value for others, imparts happiness, and positively influences the world around us.

It is the same with the joy of inner discovery. An inner discovery that we reach by ourselves certainly brings us a sense of fulfilment. But when we have friends on our journey of Truth with whom we can share the same aspirations and joys, our delight grows that much more delightful.

In these moments of happiness, even the simple presence of our companions can enlarge our sense of joy. This is how God created us. The human heart abounds with hopes and dreams of accomplishing good work for others. This desire arises from within our essence. We were imbued with it before we came into this world, so we never had to learn these feelings. They were already part of us when we were born.

Devoting our lives to creating happiness for others is the true source of the joy of living in this world. Just imagine how different your life would seem to you if you were to discover right now that your accomplishments in life had engendered misery for others. If you had lived three lives and each time had brought others more misery than joy, how would you feel about your work? Your heart would probably sink at the remorseful outcome of so many decades of life in this world. It does not matter who you are; we would all feel a dreadful emptiness and the pangs of conscience.

Within us, there pervades a belief that the supreme nature of work, and therefore our life's purpose, is to make other lives happier. We regard this as the most hallowed of human accomplishments and our most eternal endeavour.

For this reason, regardless of our past mistakes and the misery we caused others, we, as human beings, have never become too discouraged to return to this world and try again. You, too, are living in this world, right now, determined to succeed in bringing others joy. This is the real truth of human life.

I have spent several decades now writing books and speaking to audiences, and I continue to do so because seeing that my labor of love has inspired people to find their way to happiness is the source of my own delight and fulfillment. This is the reason I work. I don't work for my personal gain. Yet, what I do has brought me pure joy.

As a writer, naturally I am pleased when my books perform well and my readership expands. But the joy I feel as I write each page comes not from anticipating these results but from imagining my books reaching all my readers and bringing them gems of truth that will inspire them with inner discoveries, even if they only gain one or two helpful insights. Neither fame, recognition, nor any other material gain can give me the same spiritual delight.

I have published many books on a wide range of themes to increase the chances that my readers will pick up a book that touches their heart. When we humans go to a bookstore, we are not truly searching for a book. We are searching for the single idea that may hold the key to our happiness.

What is the happiness we seek? A multitude of people all over the world are searching for answers to their problems. My desire and my joy is to offer these people the key—the answer that will help them arrive at a solution and cultivate a happier life. This joy was my driving force through countless eons of prior lives that I dedicated to this same vocation. And you hold this same aspiration, too.

It would be most regrettable to spend our precious life in this world satisfied by other people's misery. This is a common trait of the baser inclinations of the human mind. Someone else's joy may give rise to jealous thoughts, and though we find pleasure in helping others when they are distressed, it becomes unbearable when their lives begin to improve. But such a heart only results in forlorn emptiness. It is as though we are trapped underwater and can just reach the water's surface to catch a breath of air.

We should be rich and overflowing with feelings of joy. But we limit our own happiness by holding on to the shallow belief that someone else's gain is our loss. When we see people who have found happiness in life having joyous conversations, joining diverse communities, and building wondrous societies, why should their joy make us miserable? I believe it is because we are not as happy as we should be.

Many people now believe that another country's economic gain will result in their own country's financial loss. Their perception of profit resembles a pie that has to be divided among everyone, and the only way to get a larger piece is to acquire it from someone else. This attitude has become widespread throughout the world.

I believe that this shouldn't be the way of this world. We must find positive ways to create and increase the wellspring of happiness in this world. It is possible to keep happiness in continuous supply. This is what this world needs to achieve to create societies of bounteous joy.

BECOMING A CREATOR OF HAPPINESS

A Creator of Happiness Thinks Positively

What, then, can we do to create happiness and spread it throughout the world? How do we produce societies of abundant joy?

We must begin from within each person's heart. The happiness of every individual is our starting point. In the same way that the delight of my readers has the power to infuse me with happiness, there is no mistake that happiness within each person's heart has the power to make a difference in this world.

So how do we cultivate our state of mind so that we can create happiness within our own hearts? And what can we do to impart our happiness to others? The answer is that we all need to become creators of happiness.

There are at least two steps to becoming a creator of happiness, the first of which represents what *not* to do. And that is simply to never become a creator of *un*happiness.

What is a creator of unhappiness? We can recognize creators of unhappiness by paying attention to how we feel when we spend time with the different people in our lives. Producers of unhappiness lower our spirits when we're with them. The more time we spend with them, the more miserable we feel, as though our reservoir of happiness is being drained away.

Creators of unhappiness share common traits. For example, they have a habit of talking pessimistically and going on about their complaints. They talk as though they only expect their lives to get worse, and they speak of the world as a place full of cruel and deceiving people. Associating with someone like this can be very depressing. Perhaps you can relate, from some of your own experiences.

But if we think about it, we may realize that we sometimes act like this too—perhaps not most of the time, but maybe once a year. At any rate, we've all acted like this at some point in our lives. When we're tempted to behave like a creator of unhappiness, we need to recognize the moment for what it is: a critical opportunity to gain control over our mind. We are probably right that our circumstances are unfortunate. It may be only natural to give in to the impulse to complain, dwell over our dismal situation, and wish for sympathy.

But we need to remember that people who want to improve their lot in life and guide others to do the same choose not to behave this way. Instead, they continue to smile, be positive, and think constructively, even in the midst of their sadness and distress.

Adversity Is a Treasure in Disguise

Many of the keys to a life of triumph are found precisely within difficult circumstances. Life is rich with precious experiences that allow us to develop and advance toward our goals. We encounter these experiences not only during times of ease and success, but even more so, perhaps, in times of hardship and adversity. I am not exaggerating at all.

When we are in the midst of adversity, we are surrounded by the treasures of this life, and they come in heaps so high that we can hardly find our way through them. These are extremely fortuitous circumstances, but we fail to see things in this light. We act as though we are being tortured and buried alive.

I can testify to this truth on the basis of personal experience. A large part of my philosophy, which I am sharing with all of you, did not emerge from times of happiness. Rather, these were the Truths that helped me through the most difficult periods of my life. They were the ways of thinking that helped me conquer the struggles within my mind. I am able to present them to you with such confidence because I have been through these things myself.

If only you would cast a light upon your surroundings, you would not be discovering walls deep beneath the earth. Rather, you would see mountains of glistening diamonds, sparkling gems, gleaming silver, and gold emerge before your eyes. This is what you are truly surrounded by in times of adversity. But because everything has been covered in darkness, you simply couldn't recognize how fortunate you truly were.

Adversity Shows Us Our Own Unique Purpose

This leads us to a fundamental question about life: What is the purpose of this world? What is the meaning of life?

One of the purposes of living in this world is to gain experiences that allow us to cultivate our souls. Human beings return to this world time and again. We do this to gain a variety of experiences to achieve the most essential purpose of life: to advance further in our spiritual growth.

We have all been granted a workbook of the soul. So, each time we are born, we try to choose different circumstances than before. We may, for instance, take on a different kind of occupation, a new type of environment, and different kinds of relationships. Those who have been wealthy in the past may choose to be born into poverty, and vice versa. And someone who used to enjoy good health may choose to be born with an illness.

Life always presents us with new problems and brings us only those issues that we have not wholly resolved before. Our problems would have no purpose if we had already conquered them. Your workbook was perfectly designed uniquely for you. So it will never present you with problems that are beyond your capacity, and you are the only person who can solve them.

Our hardships are our vital guides through our workbook. Therefore, as a basic rule of life, we should hold back on verbalizing our discontent, dissatisfaction, and complaints when these feelings arise. Each problem you face will have clues that will help you understand what kind of life you planned for yourself and what you truly desire to achieve in this life. The clues within our hardships help us understand who we are and what mission we are here to fulfill. We will be able to discern our unique purpose in this life; there is no need to ask a psychic to give us a reading of our future. We have the capacity to perceive on our own what purpose we wanted to serve in this life.

When you reach the conclusion of your life having conquered your problems and lived your life to the fullest, you will earn a passing grade on your workbook. The next time you revisit this world, you will no longer be solving those problems but rather helping others facing the same issues find their way to their answer. This is how our souls are given chances for further self-growth and spiritual advancement.

If this is the truth about our life in this world, then you may start to see that those of us who are presently in the middle of adversity are grappling face to face with the very purpose of our life. This is clearly not the time to turn away. We are in the midst of a rare, precious opportunity. When, in life, we come across what we believe to be a hardship or adversity that surpasses all others, this may indeed be the gift from life that was chosen just for you to best serve the cultivation of your soul. This may prove to be your most prized and valuable problem in the workbook of your life. By refusing to take on this challenge, you will be denying the most essential objective that you planned to accomplish in this life. To complain about this would be the same as spending your life carefully tracing the path of a treasure map only to fret about it when at last you discover the long-lost treasure.

Courage Is Our Sword in Adversity

Have you ever considered how much of the world's unhappiness is created and spread solely as a result of fear? It occurs frequently, to such an extent that it is unbearable to watch. In countless situations, people try to escape from the approaching flames out of pure fear of becoming engulfed by the fire. But by doing so, they allow the flames to continue burning and spread further to their surroundings.

Periods of adversity are not the times to retreat from our problems. We shouldn't even let retreat cross our mind. Times like these call for daring courage like that of Yamato Takeru. We must work up our courage and, like Yamato Takeru, draw the blade from the scabbard with a firm resolve to fight the approaching flames. With broad, audacious strokes, we must cut a path through the grass to allow the winds to blow in reverse, turning the flames toward the enemy lines.

Fires need to be quenched as soon as they arise. We must determinedly take our stand against these blazes and resolve to extinguish them immediately. It is true that, in some cases, time may be an answer. It is also true that, even if we try, we may fail to reach our answer before our life closes, but we can still gain precious experience by squarely accepting the challenges that befall us.

We Are Our Hearts and Thoughts

Our souls originally came into this world from a place in heaven in order to spend many decades of this life in our bodies. In time, we will all return again to the other world, where we will be reunited with the friends and family of our life on Earth and of our soul.

This is the time of genial conversations, when we will share the stories of our lives and especially the treasures of wisdom we have grasped through the adversity and hardships we have gone through. These are the inspiring stories of our lives that we will be able to bring with us to the other world.

The invaluable lessons of our life lie within each of our circumstances. These are the real treasures of this world, the jewels of experience that enlighten us to the truths of human life. No one's life is exactly alike. The answers that you reach are treasures that are uniquely yours, and these are the gifts that you can take with you upon your return to the other world. Those of us who have wrestled with and worked through our workbook of life will be visited by many angels and receive their praises. They will say, "You gave your life your best effort. You truly persevered, even in the face of adversity."

Are you skeptical of what I have just told you? Perhaps you are still half in doubt. So I will tell you again, with absolute certainty, that the other world exists. You have my word. Ever since I discovered the spiritual world and experienced it for myself, I have had conversations with the beings of heaven every day. So I won't hesitate to give not only my 100 percent guarantee, but even my 200 percent assurance that there is neither joke nor deception in my words. They are simply the truth.

Our only true possession in this world, the single factor that truly matters in life, is our heart, and within our heart are the inner lessons we grasped and absorbed through the effort we made to amend and cultivate our heart. It doesn't matter if we are blessed with health or stricken with illness, whether we have high social status, huge wealth, or a degree in medicine; there are no exceptions to the fact that, in time, we will all bid farewell to this world. In the other world, we will surrender all our material belongings—our glasses, wallets, and garments, everything. We will leave behind our homes, property, and, of course, our bank accounts. None of these things can be taken with us. The sole thing that will belong to us in the other world is going to be our heart.

When we accept this truth as fact, it will show us what we really need to do with our life. We will be able to discover our true purpose in life, no matter what our relationships, environment, and job may be.

Perhaps you have discovered your answer, too. In this life, there is nothing more important than to give our best effort to cultivating and polishing our mind. To accomplish this, let's throw out our negative thinking.

Let's stop thinking in pessimistic ways that could hurt or trouble others. We should no longer let ourselves utter such thoughts. I believe that this is the first step to being a creator of happiness.

The Mindset for Triumphing in Life

When we consider our life in this world with a belief in the eternal life of the soul, our perspective on life changes. We begin to notice that there are precious chances within all situations and circumstances for spiritual growth and that the purpose of our circumstances is to help us cultivate the power of what I call *invincible thinking*.

Life closely resembles a tree. There are strong winds to endure, leaves that fall, and even the dangers of withering and dying. We may struggle to gain nutrients, there may be people who try to dig up and damage our roots, and there are many other troubles that life may bring.

Regardless of all of these things, with invincible thinking, we can continue to grow upward, straight like a tree, toward the open skies. Our most essential goal is to meet the trials of life with as much wisdom and as many skills, and ideas as we can muster. With this attitude, we will be able to learn all that is possible from the trials we face and gain mastery over our time in this world. We will turn all things in life into sources of power for our soul, and ultimately, we will live a life of triumph.

The practice of reflection will help you check what kind of mental attitude you have had so far. This is a good place to begin to understand where you are and what you can do from now on to cultivate this new perspective.

CONTEMPLATION

Look back at your past, and see where you were in life...

6 months ago

_____

_____

_____

1 year ago

_____

_____

_____

2 years ago

_____

_____

_____

3 years ago

_____

_____

_____

Place yourself in these moments of the past, into your own shoes back then, and look at where you are now from each standpoint. Do you feel that you have made progress, or do you feel that you have fallen back? Has your journey been straight, or have you taken divergent paths?

If you discover that your journey so far has been fairly strong and straight, even if you had defeats and setbacks along the way, then from a broad perspective, you can be assured that you have triumphed in your life thus far.

CREATING HAPPINESS FOR OTHERS' SAKE

The first step to becoming a creator of happiness was to overcome the tendencies we may have of creating *un*happiness. Taking this step alone, however, would only put an end to our negative way of living. Not only would this result in an unexceptional life, but it would probably also be a regrettable outcome of spending so much time living in this world. We should all desire to reach higher in our accomplishments in life, to be someone who is capable of creating happiness for many people other than ourselves.

We have the opportunity to give others our help and support not only when we have achieved our own happiness, but all the time. That opportunity is in front of us no matter where we are in life; we could be in the depths of despair, at the summit of happiness, or on top of the world. No matter where we stand in our journey, we always hold the key to the gate of someone else's happiness. Those who feel that they are not ready to help others because they are grappling with their own struggles have simply not yet noticed this truth.

This is our one and only chance to live in this part of the world, in this particular time in history. Time can only march forward and bring in new ages; once this chance has gone, it will vanish forever. We are allowed only one opportunity. Never again will we have an opportunity to experience the very same relationships, in the very same places, with the very same vocation. For example, sometime in the future, you will probably come to listen to me speak again, but I will no longer be Ryuho Okawa. I will be someone completely different.

This is my reason to live every moment of my life as if it were my last chance. Each chance that comes by could be our very last. This is why it is so important to make the most of this life, giving our best, effort after effort, and to do everything we possibly can to make this life the best that it can be.

When we are in the midst of adversity, we can use those circumstances to our advantage to create something positive and good. Even if we are in the midst of our own problems, we are still capable of making others happy. If you take a moment to look around you, you'll probably find someone else who is going through the same problems as you are right now. You may also find people who will appreciate your help, regardless of how little you think you are capable of helping. If you will only give it some consideration, you will find these people around you.

A doctor who has fallen ill is still capable of helping his patients recover from their illnesses. To be able to work like this doctor just requires a shift in perspective. We simply need to see that, by shifting our concentration away from our own problems to helping the distresses that are troubling others, we will be able to notice the things that we can do or say to help them.

I have said, in the past, that it is necessary to help oneself to be capable of helping others, and my readers may wonder how they can possibly help someone else find happiness if they feel that they haven't accomplished enough of their own self-cultivation. I would like to clear up this misconception.

We shouldn't be misled by the surface-level, this-worldly meaning of the phrase *helping oneself*. What this really means is to awaken oneself spiritually. To help oneself is to try to achieve a true inner awakening, a state that is very close to true happiness, and to discover the Truths of life by reaching a deepened awareness of who we are as human beings. This is the true meaning of *helping oneself*.

Those of us who have penetrated deeply within our own heart will be able to penetrate the hearts of others. The harder we grapple with our problems, the deeper our inner awakening will be. Our understanding of what it means to be human, our perceptions of the problems we all face, and our enlightenment and insights about life will be that much more profound. These fruits of our effort lend us the ability to understand other people's struggles.

As counterintuitive as it may sound, we don't cultivate the ability to save others from their distress by living a completely worry-free and happy life. When our heart becomes too smooth and shiny, we are less capable of truly understanding sadness and pain. The truth is that we are capable of understanding others' pain because we feel our own pain. Your own pain is asking you, now that you know how it feels to face sorrow and hardship, is there really nothing you can do with this experience?

This is the question we all need to ask ourselves. I am not deliberately trying to attach a positive meaning to sorrow and hardship. However, I believe that those who have been through hardship and sorrow are capable of kindness because they are able to deeply understand other people's pain.

If this is the case, it only makes sense that struggling through hardship is a way of helping oneself to help others. And if the more deeply we delve into our own heart, the more we are capable of understanding someone else's pain, then the verbs *to understand* and *to love* mean similar things. A heart that is capable of understanding someone else's adversity is similar to a heart that treats them with love.

Some of us may believe that it requires a thorough study of the Truths to earn the right to advise and guide others about them—to practice acts of love. But the extent of this art is so limitlessly deep that it would be absurd to wait until our study is completed.

I believe that knowledge obliges action. To know the

Truths means that we must act upon them immediately. Knowledge is a requisite for action only in the sense that knowing is an essential impetus or a catalyst for action. Therefore, we shouldn't wait until we have amassed all the knowledge there is to believe that we are worthy of taking action. This work should really begin simply from our heart's desire to use our knowledge to guide others to happiness. By doing so our knowledge of the Truths will become truly useful, and only then will we also have the opportunity to truly cultivate an authentic understanding of these Truths.

Our knowledge serves as clues to help us decide what it is that we should do right now. We are capable of beginning our contribution to the movement for humankind's happiness because we have these spiritual guideposts that are now in our grasp. Through the practice of these Truths, we will cultivate a deeper knowledge and discernment that will further advance our understanding of the Truths. This elevated awareness will then lead us to seek out even more ways to make use of this new energy.

It is important, in life, to consider learning as practice and practice as learning. Both have value, and both need to be accomplished together. It is supposed to be natural that the more knowledge we gain, the more we want to act upon that knowledge. And the more of it we put into practice, the more we see that there is still much more to learn. This is a natural desire of being human.

So it is with me. Every time I speak in front of an audience, I have the opportunity to discover that there are new things I need to learn about. I am able to see that I must learn so much more of the Truths to be able to deliver teachings that will meet the needs of everyone around the world and touch each person's heart. Unless I cultivate a great range of knowledge and develop an understanding of a multitude of people's ways of thinking, I won't be able to help everyone remove the thorns from their heart. I wouldn't be able to realize these things unless I continue to speak about the Truths to more audiences.

Perhaps those who have not started to help others can claim that they are still in the middle of learning. But those who have already started, like myself, have no excuses to fall back on. I have nowhere to escape to. I can't ask to be excused by saying that I haven't learned about something yet. Giving ourselves no room for excuses, I believe, is how we are able to make our life more challenging and more meaningful to our soul.

CASTING OUR LIGHT UPON THE WORLD

I would like as many people as possible to be able to taste what it truly means *to know*. True knowledge is equivalent to enlightenment. And to achieve true enlightenment means that you are capable of change.

The basis of all enlightenment is the idea that we humans are created by our thoughts. Everything we do in this world will have begun with one thought. Therefore, our thoughts will create every action, every circumstance, and even this entire world. This is why enlightenment holds great significance in our life. Your life is the result of what you are thinking about now, and what you have been continuously thinking about thus far. So if a wonderful person is someone who is glowing with light, then the thoughts of a wonderful person must glow with light too.

You are neither your name nor your credentials, but the quality of your thoughts. The thoughts in your mind in the past, present, and future are exactly who you are. As soon as we discover this basic principle of life, it makes it difficult to allow the slightest moment of our time to go to waste. If we are our thoughts, then there is nothing more we could possibly wish to do than to create thoughts that are proper and wonderful.

But what kinds of thoughts glow with light? These are thoughts that arise from the passionate desire to bring happiness to others; they are full of goodwill. I believe that such a heart is a shining orb of love and compassion. Such a person is a divine light of this world, and to become one is the goal and desired destination of everyone in this world.

This means that no other moment can be more proper than now to look within our mind, put an end to all the dark, pessimistic thoughts that are there, and begin to fill our mind with light. When this is accomplished and the light of our heart becomes concentrated, bounteous, and so full it keeps overflowing, our mission in this life will become clear to us.

OUR MISSION
AS LIGHT

❧

What is our mission as light?

Our mission as light is to drive away the darkness.

When we, the light, allows itself to be light,

We shall be capable of banishing the darkness.

We shall be capable of dispelling the shadows.

Bringing ourselves to abounding light is of the essence.

When we acknowledge the light that exists within us

And our light bespeaks upon the world,

Our mission as light will appear of its own volition.

❧

What is our mission?

It is to bring happiness to humankind.

To bring happiness to all the billions upon this globe,

We must show them, each and all,

That their true nature is light.

❧

Before we tell them,

We must show them the meaning of light.

But if complete darkness has been prevailing,

For twenty-four hours a day, all around the world,

How can they understand the light of the sun?

We must have been through such a challenge before.

❧

If darkness has pervaded every moment
of every hour of every day,

And if only darkness has fallen in times of past,
present, and future,

Then how can they possibly perceive the world
of bounteous sunshine?

To find a way to show them is no simple endeavor.

❧

But I am certain that we will find a way.

I don't doubt that we will find the only candle

And the only match within our grasp.

I am certain that we will use this match

To set light to our candle.

Then, we shall raise it high and say to them,

"Set your eyes upon this flame, and you shall see light."

❦

Right now, this world is conquered by darkness,

But look upon the flame
of this candle that I, myself, have set alight.

This is the light.

This light may seem small and delicate,

Merely strong enough to illuminate my surroundings,

But I wish for you to fathom,

What kind of world will emerge

When this world is filled with bounteous light.

❦

Imagine what you will see

When the flame of this candle

overflows upon this world.

I will tell you that you shall see the light of day,

Like the rays of the sun cast upon the world.

You have been living within the darkness for many years,

The touches of daylight may have
vanished from your memory,

But look upon my candle,

Look upon not only my own candle,
but those of your peers.

See how your peers are also holding candles.

Imagine just how brightly we will glow if these flames
come together.

So I must tell you,

It is our mission to flood this world

with the light of our candles.

Perhaps our light won't compare

To the light of day created by the sun,
conceived originally by God's light.

But there shall be enough for all to be
set free from a world of darkness.

It is the same with our work to spread the Truths.

Since the days beyond our remembrance,

In our inner world,

The sun has never once appeared.

We have been trapped
in the world after dark.

Thus, now, more than ever,
the world is gravely in need of light.

❧

Even if our candles have only a modest glow,

There is no reason to be ashamed.

There is no reason for self-limitations.

There is no reason to despair.

It is just the beginning of all things to come.

You mustn't forget

That those who set eyes upon your light,

Will be reminded of the memories
of their original home.

Within us all, there remains

The power to believe in our hopes once more.

We must never allow a sliver of doubt,

In this power within us all
to imagine our dreams once more.

I am also not more than one glowing candle.

But, if this flame can set light to a million more candles,

Then there will be a million more candles
to cast light upon this world.

And what's more,
the light of these candles can be passed on,

And passed on again, to spread forth infinitely.

I hope you will join me on this journey
to create a world of light.

Chapter Two

LIVING

in

TRIUMPH

The soul-stirring words of this poem
are so profound that I am certain
they will serve as a wellspring of strength
and open a path forward for any heart
weighed down by distress,
exhaustion, or adversity.
You will feel these words in your heart
the moment you read this poem.

WE MUST ALL HAVE GREAT HOPE.

Let the light of God flow forth;

Let the power of God flood through;

Let the courage of God pour forth;

Let them continuously pour forth upon you.

He is the great wellspring of light,

Our ocean of wisdom,

The mountain and river of love,

And the skies of compassion.

Feel the touch of His sweet breeze as it passes by

To dry those glistening tears overcast
upon your eyes.

**YOU SHALL DREAM
OF NOTHING BUT SUCCESS.**

The defeated dreamed of defeat,

And the triumphant dreamed of triumph.

If you are going to dream,

Why not dream of victory?

Why not dream of triumph?

Why not dream of success?

Only when you have held fast to good dreams

Will triumph come to you in the fullness of time.

Living in Triumph

WE SHALL TRIUMPH OVER LIFE.

We shall realize only success.

Why do you dilly-dally?

Has dilly-dallying ever opened your path forward?

Has dwelling on problems ever led to happiness?

Roll your troubles up and toss them out the window.

Into the river they go,
the currents sweeping them far away.

Neither Truth nor light
was ever begotten of brooding.

WE SHALL BANISH PETULANCE.

We shall banish ill humor.

Who does this surly face in the mirror belong to?

A smiling countenance is most wonderful.

The peeking glow of our pearly whites

Is the boarding pass to our happiness.

Our smile has the power to
beckon more smiles onward.

WHY ARE YOU NOT MORE JOYFUL?

This morning, we awakened with life.

In the evenings, our abode awaits our return.

We have fresh air to breathe in

And lungs to breathe out.

We are blessed by lush verdure and percolating,
clean oxygen.

Our blood pulsates through our being,
infusing vitality.

WE SHOULD NEITHER OVERREACH

Nor deceive

Nor be pretentious.

There is no such need,

For we are children of God

Who shine resplendently

Just as we are.

There is no need to put on appearances.

We shall cast aside all vanity,

For children of God are already precious

Just the way we are.

WE SHALL NEVER DESPAIR,

For nothing is impossible in this world.

Hasn't humankind conceived the airplane,

Walked upon the moon,

Explored the depths of the ocean,

And driven tunnels and railways

Through mountains and every terrain?

WE MUST NOT LOSE HEART

Or become pessimistic,

For nothing is ever born of a disheartened soul,

And nothing positive is ever born of self-denial.

Put your ideas forward with determination,

Affirm your dreams with resolution

And staunchly declare,

"Yes, I can!"

WORDS ARE IMBUED WITH POWER.

We call these words *words with soul*.

Those who speak many pessimistic words

Will lead a defeated life,

Whereas positive words

Are infused with life and spirit.

Why haven't we put these words to use?

We shall speak
positively of others' lives

The way we speak positively of our own.

We shall also believe in their goodness,

For to believe in their vileness

Will lead them to disparage us.

Therefore, we shall praise them with sincerity.

The power of praise will improve their lives

As well as our very own.

WE SHALL ALWAYS TREAT
OTHERS WITH GOODWILL.

We mustn't return others' malice with our own.

We shall be suppliers of only goodwill.

Take your absolute goodwill,

Wash all evil from this world,

And fill it with abounding goodwill—

For then, indeed, we will see heaven.

We must not let work exhaust us.

Work becomes exhausting

When we regard it as selling our time.

Rather, our work should be an opportunity
to spread the Truths

And a place to meet new people.

Instead of being exhausted,

We should desire to be someone

Who searches for ways to give happiness.

**WE SHALL CHERISH EVERY MOMENT
OF OUR TIME IN THIS WORLD,**

For time is as precious as life itself.

Therefore, do not forsake your life in this world.

Hold your life dear to your heart.

Those who struggle with insomnia, rejoice!

For you are a master of creating time.

If you are fretting about troubles,

Then you have found time for self-cultivation.

LOVE WORKS LIKE OUR SAVINGS.

When we give our love to others,

We not only add this love to our own savings;

We also amass interest.

Even when we receive love from someone else,

We are being rewarded for our own virtue.

As a result, our wealth of love can only
keep growing to no end.

**WE SHALL NOT BE DEFEATED
BY ILLNESS.**

We can make the fullest
use of times of illness.

To begin with,
we now have time for inward reflection.

This may also be the chance
to become a philosopher or poet.

We can use this time to write an epic novel
and become a master novelist.

**WE SHALL NOT BE DEFEATED
BY A BROKEN HEART.**

Unrequited love begets poets,
spiritual leaders, and philosophers

And even produces
famous athletes and politicians.

So, I say, why not challenge ourselves
to break the world record

For the number of times
a heart has been broken?

DIVORCES AND REMARRIAGES
ARE TRIFLES IN LIFE.

If anything, these experiences
have enriched our lives beyond the lives of others.

You shall pay no heed
to the judgments of society.

Rather, you are the one
who can be the true expert in life

And be a beacon of light for the young.

You have become their most
valuable person there can be.

LET US ALL HUM ALONG
AS WE WALK AHEAD

And turn all ordeals into experience
and pearls of wisdom.

Let us set our foot firmly upon the earth

And walk toward the dawn on the horizon.

There is no such thing as unhappiness,

Because there is eternal life for all.

With the firm grip of our hands,

Let us grasp our happiness
as we walk forward.

Living in Triumph

Chapter Three

On the Poem

"LIVING

in

TRIUMPH"

The words of this poem are pure simplicity. To supplement them with my thoughts may only add redundancy, but I offer my thoughts nevertheless, because I would like to illuminate the themes in this poem, especially those related to the principle of courage, that are comparable to those found in New Thought philosophy. You may notice that the themes closely resemble the main concepts of this philosophy. This is because this poem was written through the divine guidance of Ameno Minakanushi, who, I believe, has captured within these verses the very essence of New Thought.

HAVE
GREAT HOPE

WE MUST ALL HAVE GREAT HOPE.

Let the light of God flow forth;

Let the power of God flood through;

Let the courage of God pour forth;

Let them continuously pour forth upon you.

He is the great wellspring of light,

Our ocean of wisdom,

The mountain and river of love,

And the skies of compassion.

Feel the touch of His sweet breeze as it passes by

To dry those glistening tears overcast upon your eyes.

❧

This verse opens by saying, "have great hope," to remind us that hope is the basis of everything in this life. That is why, to live by the New Thought philosophy, everything ultimately comes down to having hope. Hope is where our journey of light begins and also our ultimate destination. If our heart's desire truly is to live a positive life and create a shining future, then the one thing we must do beyond all else is hope for that positive life and wish for that positive future. Countless works of poetry, theory, and philosophy have tried to explain this idea.

Without a heart of hope, or at least the desire to have one, we won't have the means to embark on this journey in the first place. The philosophy of New Thought is commonly regarded as relying heavily on help from an outside power. True, there is a light above us that embraces, directs, and guides us through life. But we can only be reached if we ourselves first have hope. That is to say, we won't be able to bring light into our life without our own resolution and determination to do so. With a pessimistic mind, we react as though we desire a life of darkness, making any attempt by heaven to send us help a futile effort, no matter what means or miracles are used. This is why, our own heart, our own mind, must, before all else, resolve on a destiny of light.

On the Poem "Living in Triumph"

This resoluteness of our mind is all we need to call forth the words and light of hope that we seek. This verse promises that when we determine to hold on to our hopes, God's light and power will pour forth, not just once, but ceaselessly. When our inner world stands firmly resolved, we allow the light to reach us directly and shine straight upon us—or we may feel it springing out from within and engulfing us with its embrace. These are the moments that truly bring us the power of salvation.

Not only will we feel God's light and power pour forth; we will also be imbued with His courage. Can you tell where this courage comes from? We humans were originally fragments of God that long ago split off into unique individual souls. Therefore, though we are indeed individual beings, we are, more essentially, a part of God with His same qualities inside us. Our remembrance of this truth allows us to call forth the powerful courage of God that is already lying within our being.

Can you envision what will happen when this courage of God comes to us? As our courage rises within us, so do the wellspring of light and the ocean of wisdom, as clearly as though they have appeared before our eyes. There are reservoirs of energy, brimming to their horizons. Everywhere, we feel reserves of tremendous power and universal wisdom plenteously surrounding us. Turning our gaze above shows us great mountains and rivers of bounteous love; even the sky exudes compassion. Then, even when our eyes become misty with tears of emotion, a fresh breeze blowing by, seemingly from nowhere, helps them dry. In this way, this verse shows us how precious it is to our life to know that we are all children of God provided with the most blessed surroundings to lead a life of light.

DREAM OF SUCCESS

YOU SHALL DREAM OF NOTHING BUT SUCCESS.

The defeated dreamed of defeat,

And the triumphant dreamed of triumph.

If you are going to dream,

Why not dream of victory?

On the Poem "Living in Triumph"

Why not dream of triumph?

Why not dream of success?

Only when you have held fast to good dreams

Will triumph come to you in the fullness of time.

We are told further, in this verse, what it means to have great hope. What is great hope? It is the dream of success.

Then, in the following lines, we are told that when we fall into a defeatist attitude, it is crucial to remember that defeat is never a consequence of someone else's success over us, but only a result of our own choice to fail. If we are children of God, then no other dream but the dream of triumph befits us. So why do we hesitate to dream of triumph? Why aren't we already dreaming of success?

Defeat isn't remotely possible for those who are triumphing in life and know that they are triumphing. They are confident because they have awakened to who they are and have discovered the part of God within them. This inner knowing has given them courage. As their courage has arisen, their paths have opened wide, and these paths have promised to lead them to success.

We need to hold fast to our dreams, as continuously as possible. It is not nearly enough to merely *think* of a dream, since success cannot be created by a fleeting thought of the mind. Rather, success arises from an abiding conviction that generates an enduring motivation and desire to reach the goal. There needs to be a strong will to sustain it over time. In contrast, a motivation that cannot be sustained vanishes as soon as it emerges, and emerges and vanishes again, like the evanescence of bubbles rising to the surface; they never last long enough to bear any fruit.

TOSS YOUR
TROUBLES AWAY

WE SHALL TRIUMPH OVER LIFE.

We shall realize only success.

Why do you dilly-dally?

Has dilly-dallying ever opened your path forward?

On the Poem "Living in Triumph"

Has dwelling on problems ever led to happiness?

Roll your troubles up and toss them out the window.

Into the river they go, the currents

sweeping them far away.

Neither Truth nor light was ever

begotten of brooding.

We must not only dream of success, this verse says, but also triumph over our life—and furthermore, *realize* success. For this, in the end, should be the true purpose of our life in this world.

In our pursuit of triumph, however, we are all challenged by the stumbling blocks of life. When we run into them, we must ask ourselves whether there was ever a time when dwelling on our problems opened a path forward or made us happier people. Probably not. If we have truly awakened to our truth as a child of God and firmly resolved to rise to the occasion, we shouldn't spend our time and energy trying to resolve our problems and make them vanish; instead we should roll them up and toss them out the window.

Many of our problems are mere trifles. How much time are we wasting on brooding, dwelling, and thinking over paltry matters? How long do we want to carry them around? They only need to be tossed out at once. There is no point in fretting over trivialities—they should be tossed into the river and allowed to be washed away. The time we spend on these problems can be used elsewhere, on those things that truly advance our life.

"Neither Truth nor light was ever begotten of brooding"—there is sternness and forthrightness in these words. We have all been trapped in mental anguish at some point. It is as though we became so enamored of our pain that we could not seem to break free. But this state of fretting is really a type of self-love and self-preservation. We could have spent this time in service to others or accomplishing something positive.

When we consider our problems in this light, our time in life feels so precious that it starts to feel like a vice to spend our moments in an unconstructive way, such as loving our problems. Life gives us opportunities to choose a much higher good. And we must make the effort to take advantage of those opportunities.

CHERISH
YOUR SMILE

WE SHALL BANISH PETULANCE.

We shall banish ill humor.

Who does this surly face in the mirror belong to?

A smiling countenance is most wonderful.

The peeking glow of our pearly whites

Is the boarding pass to our happiness.

Our smile has the power to beckon more smiles onward.

Here, the poem becomes more concrete: it tells us to banish petulance and ill humor. If we take a moment to look in the mirror, we might be surprised by the sulky or morose expression that returns our gaze. Can we believe, in good conscience, that a person of such sullen mien will be able to pave the way to a bright future?

There are times when we may forget the simple beauty of a beaming smile. To fail to remember the precious worth of a smile is nearly to surrender our humanity, because a face empty of a smile is also empty of love. We might be inclined to think of giving others our love as an abstract, philosophical idea. But to give love is, in the end, as simple as showing a smile. And with each smile we give, we shall draw more smiles into the world.

The road to success begins by taking small steps, such as avoiding doting on our problems and instead cherishing our own smiles. This is the very key to the door to a bright future.

GIVE THANKS TO ALL CREATION

WHY ARE YOU NOT MORE JOYFUL?

This morning, we awakened with life.

In the evenings, our abode awaits our return.

We have fresh air to breathe in

And lungs to breathe out.

We are blessed by lush verdure and percolating,

clean oxygen.

Our blood pulsates through our being, infusing vitality.

The theme of this verse is gratitude. As humans, we are apt to take our life and all of creation for granted and forget to be grateful simply to be alive. There are so many things to be joyful and grateful for. At the end of the day, we still have a home to return to. In addition, we are surrounded by fresh air to breathe in, and our lungs work tirelessly to breathe out. So consider for a moment: Did you think to give thanks, this morning, to the life that you woke up to? Do you feel thankful, right now, regardless of the troubles and grievances of family life, that you have a family and home to welcome you? Have you ever felt grateful simply to be breathing? Those who bemoan their misfortune and wallow in misery have forgotten the heart of gratitude.

We owe gratitude for our health and vitality to all those things. But have you ever thought further, about where our precious oxygen comes from? Have you thought to give thanks to those who sustain the pure air we breathe? Pure oxygen is always in full supply; never has it been completely depleted. And this we owe to the bounteous foliage of nature. Their oxygen nourishes our lifeblood and circulation; they are our very source of life and vitality. The emerald mountains and green pastures that abound around us create the air we breathe. Without them, there would be no one to replenish our supply of pure oxygen, our vital source of vigor and vitality.

CAST ASIDE VANITY

WE SHOULD NEITHER OVERREACH

Nor deceive

Nor be pretentious.

There is no such need,

For we are children of God

Who shine resplendently

Just as we are.

There is no need to put on appearances.

We shall cast aside all vanity,

For children of God are already precious

Just the way we are.

Those who rush to succeed by pushing beyond their true capacity, deceiving, or putting on airs have forgotten that everything we need is already provided by God. This kind of behavior comes from the wrong kind of self-reliance—a belief that our ability alone can open all doors to our future, or a belief that we achieve success solely by ourselves.

Everything about our lives—our beginnings, our preconditions, and our foundations—has been rendered to us by God. Our own task, then, is to find a way to weave these circumstances together so they may blossom into the world. To this end, everything that we will ever need as our foundation has been delivered upon us by God. Those who overreach, deceive, or put on airs have lost sight of the fact that we have been blessed with all of creation to sustain and nurture our lives. So if we find ourselves doing these things, we must consider whether we have become needlessly absorbed in making our own lives shine forth. Until we're able to appreciate the blessings we've been given, we won't be able to truly understand that we are children of God.

We have always had an inner self of resplendence, and it is essential that we recognize how brilliantly our inner self glows. Our inner light is not at all like the preordained wattage of a light bulb or a fluorescent tube. How dimly their lights glow, compared with the limitless voltage that we humans can endure! We can generate a resplendence that illuminates endlessly.

When we are told that we are shining brightly just as we are, it does not mean that we should be fully content with our current state in life. It is not meant to have passive overtones. It is really asking us to notice the light of our true potential that we already possess within ourselves. This is the very mark of being a child of God. Because this is our nature, we don't need to put on appearances or pretentions. That is why we should always remember that we are children of God and precious to begin with, just the way we are.

Some people, when they are told this, fall into an abyss of despair and self-loathing. The next verse speaks to those people.

NEVER DESPAIR

WE SHALL NEVER DESPAIR,

For nothing is impossible in this world.

Hasn't humankind conceived the airplane,

Walked upon the moon,

Explored the depths of the ocean,

And driven tunnels and railways

Through mountains and every terrain?

On the Poem "Living in Triumph"

We must never despair, lose faith in our own worth, or believe we are incapable of making anything of our lives. We are, indeed, children of God, just the way we are. But by precisely the same token, we are also endowed by the God-given capacity to contrive and conceive who we are. As the history of human feats has shown, nothing is impossible for us. Humans can now fly, walk the moon, traverse the bottom of the ocean, and furrow the earth. These were all once believed to be beyond human reach.

Imagine the zeal of Icarus, who dreamed of flying with such eagerness that, as legend holds, he fell to his death when the wax holding his wings together melted away. Thousands of years later, humankind has made his dream come true. Not only that, but we have also traveled to the moon, made discoveries on the ocean floor, and even tunneled through mountains to lay railways.

Therefore, this strong belief that we are children of God with an inner luminescence will never lead to inactivity. This is a belief in ourselves as light, and as light, we also desire to use our ingenuity to grow our resplendence toward greater lengths and farther heights—as far and wide as possible— to reach the worlds that lie beyond. This is the mission that we human beings have promised to undertake, and with this strong resolve, nothing is impossible.

DECLARE "I CAN!"

WE MUST NOT LOSE HEART

Or become pessimistic,

For nothing is ever born of a disheartened soul,

And nothing positive is ever born of self-denial.

Put your ideas forward with determination,

Affirm your dreams with resolution

And staunchly declare,

"Yes, I can!"

Even if we conquer despair, our mind may continue to struggle with other negative states, such as pessimism and self-denial. So how should we deal with these feelings? The answer this verse gives is, "Nothing is born of a disheartened soul. Nothing positive is born of self-denial."

We shouldn't forget God's essential reason for creating us. He wished to nurture us, and He imbued us with a purpose: to accomplish remarkable feats in this world in His stead. If we are disheartened about ourselves, it means that we have forgotten that we are His children and that, moreover, we have forsaken and turned a deaf ear to His expectations for us as children of God.

So when we feel we have lost faith in ourselves, we must take these words to heart: "Nothing positive is born of self-denial." It is remarkable how often we believe we are unequal to our tasks and allow self-imposed limitations to discourage us from trying. We need to consider whether these thoughts truly serve our true nature as children of God.

We engage in self-denial because our hearts have become hardened into a state of self-pity, a concern for our own well-being. But the true purpose of our lives is not to serve ourselves. Our lives are God's lives, and our work is God's work. We belong in this world to serve God.

The only answer to our pessimism and self-denial is to accept this purpose and proclaim it as fact, in the manner that these lines describe: "Put your ideas forward with determination, affirm your dreams with resolution, and staunchly declare, 'Yes, I can!'"

Every person, event, and circumstance that obstructs us and seems to impede our way forward is only an illusion conceived by our own faint heart. If, right now, we believe anyone to be obstructing our advancement in life, we need to consider whether they really are. Is it possible that these circumstances have instead manifested from our own inner desires? Could this situation be happening because our hearts have cowered, we lack courage, and we are afraid of advancing straight ahead and so hope that someone will interfere and deny us a path forward?

When we truly discover our mission and we become infused with our true strength, everyone in this world will turn into our supporters. If we consider those around us to be our foes, not friends, it may mean that somewhere in our heart we are still denying our future and that this denial is being projected into the world around us. That is why, to conquer our self-denial, we need to have a strong spirit and be able to declare that we can achieve our dreams.

WIELD
THE POWER
OF WORDS

WORDS ARE IMBUED WITH POWER.

We call these words *words with soul.*

Those who speak many pessimistic words

Will lead a defeated life,

Whereas positive words

Are infused with life and spirit.

Why haven't we put these words to use?

Words are a gift God gives to humankind to show us that we are spiritual beings. Even though we humans came from heaven, our true original home, these memories of our home and our true essence faded away when we came into this world.

God did not wish to forsake us, however; so he gave us the power of words as clues to help us regain these lost memories. By seeing the way that the words we think and speak become reality exactly the way they are expressed, our memories are triggered, and we are reminded of the power of creation that God has infused into our essence. Our words are God's divine weapons, the divine sword of courage, and they are gifted from Him as a token of love to prove that we are children of God. The words we speak have this creative power, and so a life of many pessimistic words can bring defeat, and a life filled with positive words can bring success.

Where we are today is the outcome of the sum of all of our words, which became the building blocks of our human character and determined the degree of our current success. If we have not been able to open a path to success yet, the basis of the cause is usually our words. We should look back over our life during the past several decades and reflect on the words we have spoken. We are solely responsible for our own inability to make the most of our weapons—our words—to reach success.

GIVE PRAISE

WE SHALL SPEAK POSITIVELY OF OTHERS' LIVES

The way we speak positively of our own.

We shall also believe in their goodness,

For to believe in their vileness

Will lead them to disparage us.

Therefore, we shall praise them with sincerity.

The power of praise will improve their lives

As well as our very own.

So many methods of success that are practiced in the real world only seek advancement for ourselves, and not for others, and give little consideration to the trouble and hurt we cause or how much we are taking advantage of others. In contrast, this verse says that we shouldn't only be satisfied by improving our own life. This verse represents the aspect of love in the teachings of New Thought, which attests to the fact that New Thought is not just a shallow system of self-realization and success. I would like more people to become aware that New Thought is founded on the basis of love—love for others as well as ourselves as children of God. As this verse shows, the philosophy of New Thought is not based on fancy but on teachings that are comparable to Buddhist and Christian principles. In this respect, nothing truly separates the beliefs of Christianity, Buddhism, and Shintoism from one another.

The essence of New Thought is a belief in making other people's lives positive as well as our own. We must beware: to misunderstand or forget this will lead to our own demise. What we should do is to "praise them with sincerity," and let the power of words work their own magic.

When we are able to offer praise, it is an indication that our state of mind has reached the status of a "supplier" of love. And as we continue our work to distribute love to more people, our inner capacity and human character will also grow together, and as a result, our desire to benefit others will end up benefiting ourselves, too.

TREAT OTHERS WITH ABSOLUTE GOODWILL

**WE SHALL ALWAYS TREAT
OTHERS WITH GOODWILL.**

We mustn't return others' malice with our own.

We shall be suppliers of only goodwill.

Take your absolute goodwill,

Wash all evil from this world,

And fill it with abounding goodwill—

For then, indeed, we will see heaven.

❧

To praise others with sincerity is essentially to treat others with goodwill no matter what the circumstances may be. To return someone's malice with malice of our own makes us unexceptional people. In fact, it makes us baser than the ordinary person, because it is a deed that forsakes our pride as a child of God.

If someone treats us with ill will, we should answer with *good*will; Jesus Christ preached the same principle. We would have ill will everywhere if we were to add further malice onto the ill will we receive. What good could that bring? It wouldn't make our lives better, and neither would it improve the world.

It should be our goal to be a supplier of goodwill instead. If the notions of *loving others* and *giving others love* are too large to grasp and put into practice, then remember to be a *supplier of goodwill*. The absolute goodwill of our work will help wash away evil from this world, and when good prevails, a heaven will emerge upon Earth.

GIVE HAPPINESS
EVERY DAY

WE MUST NOT LET WORK EXHAUST US.

Work becomes exhausting

When we regard it as selling our time.

Rather, our work should be
an opportunity to spread the Truths

And a place to meet new people.

Instead of being exhausted,

We should desire to be someone

Who searches for ways to give happiness.

❧

Most of us are inclined to think of showing others love and compassion as something that we do separately from day-to-day life, perhaps on special occasions. But that approach won't lead to the royal road of life. Our true sanctum of practicing love and compassion is where we spend most of our time each day, and God builds his sacred temple in the same place to foster us through life.

As long as we think of work as a business transaction in which we sell our time, our work will feel draining to us. It is, instead, a place of holy work where there are opportunities to spread happiness to those we encounter every day. The life of the most exceptional, talented, and knowledgeable person would come to naught without the relationships that we humans form throughout life. What use would our knowledge and talents be if we spent life completely alone? What purpose can having a good-natured personality serve if we don't share it with others? We should be thankful to have a way to use our abilities as we interact with many people.

We are here to give happiness not to those who live far away, who are complete strangers, or who live elsewhere in the world, but to the people we meet every day. These are the people, above all others, with whom we should begin our work of giving happiness.

CHERISH EVERY MOMENT OF TIME

WE SHALL CHERISH EVERY MOMENT
OF OUR TIME IN THIS WORLD,

For time is as precious as life itself.

Therefore, do not forsake your life in this world.

Hold your life dear to your heart.

Those who struggle with insomnia, rejoice!

For you are a master of creating time.

If you are fretting about troubles,

Then you have found time for self-cultivation.

❦

Time is the essence of life. Although we think of time as a measure of the day passing by, it is far more precious than this; time is life itself. The passing of time is our very breath of life. Time that is wasted, therefore, is life we have forsaken. This is why we must cherish every moment.

And if you need to see proof to believe this, imagine what would happen if time were to freeze. If the Universe stopped the flow of time right now, do you believe that life would continue? Or, imagine what would have happened before the dawn of humankind if time had frozen when God dispersed His light to create human souls. Would you and I be here at this very moment?

Sleepless nights are a joyful blessing that have turned us into experts at creating further time. So if we are fretting over any troubles, we can use that time for something else useful; we can invest our time in preparing for what lies in our future.

BE A WELLSPRING
OF LOVE

LOVE WORKS LIKE OUR SAVINGS.

When we give our love to others,

We not only add this love to our own savings;

We also amass interest.

Even when we receive love from someone else,

We are being rewarded for our own virtue.

As a result, our wealth of love can
only keep growing to no end.

When love is created, it will eventually conceive children
of its own. It works actively the moment it is brought forth
to the world to produce more good. No matter where it is,

where it was conceived, or where it is intended to go, love will keep benefitting other people. It will continue to create the kind of "profit" that benefits others, in the spiritual meaning of the word *profit* as something with value.

So, the work to create love holds precious value in this world. We should aim to be like love that drifts anywhere in the world, like a floating balloon, that will always produce good regardless of where it journeys. And for this reason, there is no true need for us to think about where our love will go.

NEVER GIVE IN TO DEFEAT

WE SHALL NOT BE DEFEATED BY ILLNESS.

We can make the fullest use of times of illness.

To begin with, we now have time
for inward reflection.

On the Poem "Living in Triumph"

This may also be the chance

to become a philosopher or poet.

We can use this time to write an epic novel

and become a master novelist.

This verse brings up illness, one of the hardships of life. Most of us perceive illness as an obstruction, something that hampers the course of our life. But is that really what it is? In illness, we create time. This time can be used and turned to our fullest advantage.

Some people may frivol away much of this time in debating whether illness does or doesn't exist. But if we are ill, what matters is that we use this circumstance to its fullest potential. By doing so, we will make so much use of our time that it will be as if we weren't really ill. Illness offers us a valuable opportunity for deep inward reflection and may even turn us into a philosopher, poet, or great writer. This is the principle of self-reflection within New Thought in which the practice of positive thinking and invincible thinking coincide, and I believe that this principle deserves notice.

WE SHALL NOT BE DEFEATED BY A BROKEN HEART.

Unrequited love begets poets,

spiritual leaders, and philosophers

And even produces famous athletes and politicians.

So, I say, why not challenge ourselves

to break the world record

For the number of times a heart has been broken?

Perhaps you understand how it feels to have a broken heart. This verse says, "Unrequited love begets poets, spiritual leaders, and philosophers, and even produces famous athletes and politicians." This is a gospel truth of life that not only characterizes an ordeal like heartbreak, but also the other possible kinds of setbacks in life. Every setback we ever face is a springboard of life in disguise. Each is an ordeal that we can always turn around into an asset. When we are able to rise to the occasion and turn adversities into opportunities, we are truly strengthened and gain many times more power than we originally possessed. Therefore, it is essential to our lives to know that times of hardship and adversity are indeed not what they seem; they are catalysts, stepping-stones, or vaulting-horses for cultivating the soul.

The purpose of a vaulting horse is to lift you to the skies. It is not meant to be an obstruction or an impediment; thus, if this is all you can see in your circumstances, you are actually the one who is deeming yourself unfit to fly. We don't want to make this mistake. So, rather than spend our time sulking over our heartbreak, we should dare ourselves to break the world record for the number of times our heart has been broken.

DIVORCES AND REMARRIAGES
ARE TRIFLES IN LIFE.

If anything, these experiences have enriched
our lives beyond the lives of others.

You shall pay no heed to the judgments of society.

Rather, you are the one who can be
the true expert in life

And be a beacon of light for the young.

You have become their most
valuable person there can be.

This verse talks about divorce and remarriage, which are very common these days. I believe that, regardless of how society may perceive them, these experiences enrich our lives beyond the lives of others.

We are distressed, ultimately, because we allow ourselves to be concerned about how society judges us. We don't want to be thought of as a failure of a wife and mother or husband and father. But just consider: How will we be able to give advice and guidance to anyone else if we are empty of the experiences that cultivate human wisdom? What insight can we give to the suffering and distressed if we have never gone through any hardship or sorrow of our own? Clearly, these experiences enhance our wisdom well beyond that of others.

You won't need to tell all or reveal all the things that you have been through. But your experiences will perfume your wisdom with the hints of its own aroma and textures when you offer others your guidance and advice. This is the way that the masters of life have been created. Divorce and remarriage are the precious experiences that grow us into the most valuable person that a youth can have in his or her life.

BELIEVE THAT THERE IS NO SUCH THING AS UNHAPPINESS

LET US ALL HUM ALONG AS WE WALK AHEAD

And turn all ordeals into experience

and pearls of wisdom.

Let us set our foot firmly upon the earth

And walk toward the dawn on the horizon.

There is no such thing as unhappiness,

Because there is eternal life for all.

With the firm grip of our hands,

Let us grasp our happiness as we walk forward.

I hope that this last verse has inspired your heart to hum along your journey through life and has instilled you with a resolve to transform all your circumstances into your own experience and pearls of wisdom.

There is nothing in this world that can truly harm us, nor can anyone be our foe, because God sends everything as an experience that can be turned into our jewels, gems, and light of wisdom. We will then have these to pass on to others through acts of nurturing love and guidance. This is how our practice of giving love truly begins. Setbacks and failures are essential for our growth into someone who is capable of helping others. They are vital stepping-stones that allow us to develop and evolve further. They are mountain trails that bring us the delight of being of service to others. Therefore, we face setbacks and failures not because we are being tortured and life is being cruel, but because they allow us to become envoys of nurturing love and forgiveness.

The verse says that each foot forward must be set down firmly. It is important for us to hold a firmly grounded perception of life. That is to say, to realize our hopes, we need to face reality squarely, ascertain the circumstances, study them from different angles, and find the way to break down and break through these walls right from within them. I cannot emphasize enough how important it is to tread with not a light-hearted, but a grounded footing and without any pretentions about our own knowledge or conceptions.

We must walk tenaciously on this journey toward the rising sun. This sunrise represents the hope that opened the beginning of this poem. It is the individual hopes that each of us holds and is trying to fulfill.

The conclusion of "Living in Triumph" is the last part of this verse, which says that there is no such thing as unhappiness. This is saying that unhappiness is just an illusion within our mind that will vanish the moment we believe that it doesn't exist. Even if it were to exist in reality, it is actually food for the soul. It holds precious nutrients that nourish our body and circulation. By taking in these nutrients, we will be able to make unhappiness disappear, as if it never existed.

We can also roll up unhappiness and throw it out the window. Unhappiness is, in reality, as fragile as the morning mist that can be cleared away by the slightest breeze to reveal the vast, open sky. Since there is power in our words, we must use them bravely to blow away the encroaching unhappiness.

We human beings have eternal life, and we should never forget that this is a cause for rejoicing, because it lets us see every circumstance that life gives us as an opportunity to learn something valuable. And when we consider life from this eternal standpoint, we understand that there truly is no such thing as unhappiness. No matter how we may stumble through our journey, our experiences are precious lessons of life that show us the ways that we humans make mistakes so that our mistakes may become our wisdom in our next life. When we have grasped with our hearts this truth about unhappiness, we will have firmly grasped hold of happiness. And from the moment that we determine to reach forward with our hands, we can only triumph.

Chapter Four

CREATING
YOUR OWN
DESTINY

WHAT IT MEANS
TO BE HUMAN

Have you ever wondered what the purpose of the spiritual training we go through in life is? The Shinto god Ameno Minakanushi says that our goal is to know the nature of human beings and that discovering human nature is our duty. Ameno Minakanushi says that human nature is defined by two characteristics.

The first characteristic is our ability to bring happiness to others. He is saying not just that it is good to bring happiness to others, but that it is part of the human condition to bring happiness to others. This is a revolutionary idea. Spreading happiness is not an ideal to which we should aspire, but is part of our essential nature as human beings. This is a type of divine concept that comes down from heaven for human beings to simply accept. If we are convinced that we are here to bring happiness to others, we will see the world around us in a completely different way. This idea definitely has the power to bring positive changes to the world.

The second characteristic of human nature as defined by Ameno Minakanushi is our potential for infinite growth and development. The more happiness we can create, the more growth we can achieve—and there's no limit to how much we can grow. We are blessed with this potential because we are here to bring happiness to others. In other words, our infinite potential doesn't mean that we can act irresponsibly as we please—it means that our nature is to improve ourselves in ways that bring happiness to others.

This concept of human nature flatly denies the false self and the idea that we must clear our clouded minds through the practice of introspection. If creating happiness is part of what it means to be human, then anyone who is egocentric or who harbors thoughts that harm others does not even qualify as human. This may sound harsh, but this unique and powerful idea can help us focus on our potential as human beings; it gives us no option but to grow.

THE NATURE
OF GOD

When we become aware of these essential characteristics of human beings—bringing happiness to others and growth—we can start to recognize and decipher the nature of God. God's nature is defined by three main qualities.

The first is *illumination*: God shines light on the world. The light of God lets us recognize our true self, our original state as a child of God. It shows us the brilliance of our true nature. We all have a diamond-like nature within us, but this inner diamond can shine and its beauty can be appreciated only when it is illuminated by God's light. It is the nature of God to shine His light on the world, revealing its beautiful, true nature.

God's second quality is *energy*: God endows all creatures with life force. The nature of God is to give life to all things, nurture them, and make them prosper. Without this source of energy, all creation—humans, animals, and plants—would only decline. It is God's life energy that lets all things prosper and develop.

God's third quality is *hope*. It is God's nature to strive to bring infinite good to the world. God is fundamentally hopeful, and decline, destruction, and decay are not part of God's nature. Hope is the very purpose of God's existence. God exists for the sake of bringing happiness to all creation; this shows how generous God is.

God is the light that shines on the world. He is the life force that nurtures all life, and He is hope itself. This is the very essence of God. He possesses overwhelming power, light, and goodness. What then is the essence of light? The following verse contemplates the theme of light.

THE ESSENCE
OF LIGHT

Never forget that light is a product of positive intention.

Darkness is never the essence of God.

God did not create darkness at the time of creation.

Darkness is merely a product of chance.

Darkness only appears as a result of chance.

Light is not a product of chance.

It is the nature of light that it exists.

It is the nature of light that it shines.

❧

Never forget that light is a product of positivity,
but darkness is a product of negativity.

Remember that light was created by God's Will,
but darkness is a product of chance.

Remember that goodness is a positive existence,
but evil is a negative existence.

Because God is goodness itself,
God gives us energy.

Light is the energy of life.

Light is the beacon that illuminates the world.

Light is hope.

Light is development.

Light is goodness.

Light is a guide.

Light is the courage to live.

To know Light is to know your true nature,
for you are a child of Light.

Humans are children of Light.

Seek the essence of this Light.

Explore the essence of this Light.

Discover what Light is.

Walk with the Light.

March in the midst of Light.

Advance under the Light.

Lead your life in the time of Light.

Live with the Light.

Act in concert with the Light.

Let the Light kindle the torch within you.

Let the Light nourish your heart.

Let the Light become the purpose of your life.

Let the Light bring out the life of God,
the breath of God.

Let the Light be the greatest feat of your life.

The theme of this verse follows the same line of thought as the New Thought philosophy introduced by American thinkers such as Ralph Waldo Emerson. This idea represents the monistic view of the world, which states that only light truly exists. In this view, evil is the absence of good, just as cold is the absence of heat. This is the truth of our existence from the perspective of the spirit world, but it can be quite difficult for us to apply this perspective to the things that happen in the physical world around us.

Divine spirits in the higher world of heaven can really feel how true these words are. The Shinto god Ameno Minakanushi, who inspired me to write this verse, has been living in the higher heaven (the World of Tathagatas in the eighth dimension) for the last three thousand years, so he has probably forgotten the physical senses. Residing in heaven, he probably keenly feels how true this verse is, and he probably sees no point in the duality of good and evil. But as physical beings living in this world, we need to take this view with a grain of salt.

Still, this viewpoint can help us achieve our goals. It makes us think about what our goal is and what our ideal self is, and it shows us how we can start thinking to achieve these goals. This is a powerful thought that we cannot simply overlook.

Within this verse, we find profound Truths that are powerful enough to form the basis of a spiritual movement that can attract and influence a lot of people. These spiritual inspirations are now sent from heaven to guide people to true happiness and to create a better world.

THE POWER OF DREAMS

Dreaming is truly invaluable.

The ability to dream is the proof that
we are blessed with the same creative freedom as God's.

Fly in your dreams.

Expand yourself in your dreams.

Live your life to the fullest in your dreams.

Do not limit yourself in your dreams.

Creating Your Own Destiny

Always hold a dream in your heart.

When you no longer dream, your spirit has died.

When you no longer dream, your spirit has aged.

Don't allow yourself to become decrepit.

Preserve eternal youth.

Eternal youth is the ability to dream.

Eternal youth is the power to embrace dreams.

Limiting your dreams limits yourself.

Never be ashamed of your ability
to envision grand dreams.

Be proud of your ability to dream big.

Lamenting failure comes from abandoning dreams.

But many underdogs do not realize
that they have abandoned their dreams.

Never be deluded by reality.

Never be deluded by results.

Do not fear unfavorable outcomes.

Rather, lament your inability to hold on to your dreams.

Do not seek results— they will be given to you.

Accept the results quietly when they are given to you.

Cherish your dreams.

Keep pursuing your dreams.

Creating Your Own Destiny

But do not attach conditions
about when or how they should come true.

When they are given to you,
accept them with great gratitude.

This is a secret of life.

Dreams represent hope, which is one of the characteristics of God. Ameno Minakanushi knows that we face many difficult challenges in this world. But he wants us to use the power of dreams to overcome these challenges. As long as we believe in the light and see human beings as fundamentally good, we can find ways to achieve happiness in this world—through our ability to dream.

He is saying we should not limit our dreams, but become limitless in our dreams. We should believe in our boundless dreams. As long as we keep on believing in our dreams and taking action to make them come true, we will always find a way to achieve them. When we lose our dreams, we've become old. But as long as we keep pursuing our dreams, we will remain young. Reading these powerful words to yourself should fill you with strength.

These divine words of inspiration penetrate into our inner hearts; they are apodictic just like the words in the Book of Psalms. We can feel the authority of divine spirits behind these words. The simplicity and elegance of these words prove that they do not come from a physical person living in this world, but a divine spirit in a higher world of heaven.

This verse also tells us what the ultimate state of happiness is. Those who have failed in life have often shuttered their own dreams. For them, dreams are as ephemeral as soap bubbles; they let their dreams become crushed just as easily as they let bubbles burst. People who see themselves as losers are often trapped in the perspective of their present situation. They only believe when they see favorable results, and they stop believing when they are faced with unfavorable results. But living like this is far from living in the world of faith.

We may not realize just how powerful dreams can be, because there's really no way to measure our ability to dream. But there are actually differences in our ability to dream. Just as there are different ranks in calligraphy and judo, and just as some people are better drivers than others, in the world of the mind, too, we may be better or worse at embracing dreams. Some may be experts at following their dreams, while others may be beginners.

From the perspective of highly skilled experts, many people may seem to get stuck and feel lost over trifling matters and so give up on their dreams too easily. We can cultivate our ability to dream by dreaming big and by continuing to dream until our dreams come true. The path to success will open before us when we improve our dreaming ability to a professional level.

We should not allow ourselves to be deluded by results. We should not allow ourselves to become realists in a negative sense. Even if our wishes do not come true in the way we wanted them to, it does not mean that all the doors of possibility have been shut.

I once received a spiritual message from heaven that said, "When one door of fate closes, another one opens." This is very true. The verse above is expressing the same idea. When a door shuts in front of you, you naturally think that you won't be able to enter—but another door is guaranteed to open. This is the truth. What matters is finding the opening door and entering through it. If you give up on your dream when the first door closes, you are only believing in the results you can see with your eyes, and you are not trusting the invisible world.

We do not have to "attach conditions about when or

how they should come true" if we are firmly convinced that another door will open when one door closes. There will always be a new door opening before you, if you just believe. If you keep looking, you will find a number of new paths that will lead you to your dreams.

Destiny has numerous scenarios ready for each one of us. The first scenario may be the one we will live out if we allow our circumstances to decide the course of our life. But the second, third, or fourth scenarios will be given to us if we decide to use our willpower to change our destiny and open up a new path.

So even if a door closes, keep looking. The original door may have been at the back of the hall, while the next one may be at the front, allowing you to find the best seat. This kind of thing is very common. So don't let self-limitation limit your dreams.

Authoring Our
Own Life Story

God wishes for us to develop and grow so that we can each become the author of our life. He wants each of us to create our own story, our own unique drama, but at the same time, he wants us to work together to create a beautiful story on a societal, national, and global scale. God Himself is an artist; He is the executive producer of the grand play that is unfolding on Earth, and he wishes each one of us to play the leading role in the story of our life.

The first scene of the drama of our life begins the moment we are born into this world. We start from scratch, and we learn as we grow up. As we gain knowledge and experience, we open up a new path for ourselves that allows us to edify others.

We are blessed to be able to choose the role we play in our life. If life were a TV drama, we would be assigned a certain role, and we wouldn't be able to change our role in the middle of the show. But in the drama of life, we can choose the role we like, and we can even switch our role and choose who will play the supporting roles.

Some people may feel that they can only play a supporting role and plan on ending their life as a supporting character even in their own life story. But once they experience a spiritual awakening or encounter spiritual Truths, they can transform themselves to play the starring role and start living a completely new life. We are blessed with infinite possibilities as we author our life story.

THE SWORD
OF COURAGE

When obstacles surround you,
you may feel as though there's nothing you can do
except sit and await your death.

But stay undaunted.

Unsheathe your sword resolutely.

Take courage, and slash down the surrounding grass.

Creating Your Own Destiny

At that time, a wind will blow from the east and
help you open your way through your fate.

❧

When fate requires you to rise up,
stand up against your fate.

Stand firm like the guardian of the temple.

Cut off your own retreat.

Do not withdraw, but march forward determinedly.

Cut your way through with your sword of courage.

Only with such strong mettle and endeavor
can you change your destiny greatly.

A streak of courage
will lead you to the path of greatness.

❧

Courage is the driving force for happiness. This verse tells a
story of the ancient Japanese hero and Shinto god Yamato

Takeru and shows us the nature of courage. Walking across a grassy plain on his way to an expedition, Yamato Takeru was surrounded by his enemy, who trapped him by setting fire to the grass around him. But he took out his miraculous sword, Kusanagi, and used it to cut away the burning grass. Just then, a strong wind sprang up and turned the fire toward his enemy, allowing Yamato Takeru to escape. This story is a good example of how we can use courage to open up our own destiny. Although it seems as though the wind saved him, it was actually his courage that saved his life.

Courage is an indispensable element in accomplishing great works. All of us can muster up courage, but few have actually done so. Just like the ability to embrace a dream, courage is one of the latent capabilities that exist within all of us. But the vast majority of people live out their lives without ever calling upon this latent power.

The miraculous sword of Yamato Takeru is a symbol of the latent power of courage. Each one of us has our own sword of courage. All the obstructions that block our way disappear when we draw this sword, stand firm, and cut our way through our own destiny.

When we suffer from a sense of failure or frustration, we feel as if we are being tossed about by circumstances, trapped in our current situation. But we often forget that we are wearing a sword of courage. Draw that sword, fight your way through, and open up a way in front of you. A way will open for those with strong resolve.

This holds true in any life situation. Those who face difficult situations in business may feel desperate and start worrying aloud about going bankrupt. But they can find a way out of their situation if, instead of lamenting and moaning about it, they take out their sword of courage, stand up resolutely, and do everything they can to carve their own path. A path opens before us when we make every effort and try every means—for example, meeting as many people as possible. Most people give up before even trying. But a crisis is exactly the time when we need to give it our all.

Our gender or age should not limit our ability to muster courage. This is proven by the French heroine, saint, and military leader Joan of Arc, also known as "the maid of Orleans." She was only sixteen years old when she summoned her courage to save her country. Her accomplishment shows that whether we are young or old, male or female, it is possible for all of us to take courage. This is the key to bringing happiness to the world.

Joan of Arc, a Girl Who Saved Her Country

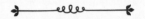

Joan of Arc was born into a farming family in Domremy, France, in 1412. At an early age, Joan started hearing voices and having mystical visions. When she was seventeen, she received a divine message telling her to liberate Orleans and save France by expelling the invading English army. Dressed in white armor and riding a white horse, she led the French troops to Orleans. After two years of fierce battles, she led the French army in a momentous victory and liberated Orleans. Although she saved France, the Catholic Church subjected her to the Inquisition. After being interrogated more than a dozen times, she was found guilty of heresy and burned at the stake. She has long been considered one of history's greatest saints, who liberated France and protected its independence. Although it was obvious to everyone that she was a messenger from heaven who carried out a sacred mission of saving France, it took more than five hundred years for the Roman Catholic Church to canonize her as a saint.

THE CONTINUITY
OF LOVE

Do you find meaning in your ordinary life?

Love is what brings meaning into everyday life.

The nature of love is an abiding feeling for others
that lasts through life's monotonous days.

Look at the sun.

Does it not do the same mundane task of
shining down upon us every day?

We must realize that
it is the sun's incessant, everyday work
that grows plants and nurtures humans.

Adversities are like the knots of a tree.

Although they temper its mettle,
knots alone do not make up the whole tree.

A tree also needs steady, simple growth.

Cherish your ordinary days.

Treasure your everyday life.

Embrace your day-to-day relationships.

Love those you meet in your daily life.

Love is not mere passion.

Love is not only about caring for those in pain.

Within love reside perseverance and endurance.

What hardships are involved in
loving a miserable person?

Creating Your Own Destiny

The inexhaustible energy that keeps nurturing people
is the true essence of love.

❧

If courage is the power that lets us stand up resolutely in
the face of adversity, love is the power that lets us endure
an uneventful life. Even those who can draw their sword
of courage in times of pain or distress may find it difficult
to take control of their destiny in their everyday life.
Mundanity may well be the biggest enemy we face in life.
Bringing meaning to a seemingly mundane life can be a
lot more difficult than we think.

Great figures appear in times of hardship, but the
greatest figures appear in ordinary life. They demonstrate
their greatness by their tireless efforts to shine light and
offer love. It certainly is a brave act to sacrifice yourself to
save other people's lives, but it is as difficult to continue
giving love to others over the course of an ordinary life.
Continuing to love is indeed a courageous act.

Take these words to heart: *Love's strength is tested
in an ordinary life. Love shines through perseverance and
endurance.* We may seek a burning, passionate love. Or we
may feel that love is about extending a helping hand to

the sufferer. You can certainly find the radiance of love in passion and the beauty of love in compassion. But the hardest kind of love to offer is the simple, ceaseless love for others in an ordinary, everyday life.

It would certainly be very dramatic if the sun only shone when the earth entered a glacial period. But of course, this isn't what we want, because then all creation would cease to exist. We survive because the sun shines constantly, every day.

Discover the essence of love in the sun. Shine your light and brighten up your everyday life just like the sun.

THE
RESPONSIBILITY
TO PROSPER

Prosperity is more the nature of God
than an attribute of God.

God is prosperity itself.

Prosperity is God Himself.

Human beings are children of God.

As His children, humans have
the same nature of growth and prosperity.

Forgetting this truth is the source of unhappiness.

Human beings have a responsibility to prosper.

When we become aware of this,
trifling misdeeds and miserable feelings will vanish.

They will disappear like dew in the morning sun.

Listen to the voice from heaven.

It is your responsibility to prosper.

God has endowed you with this duty.

So fulfill your responsibility.

Carry out your duty.

Humans are warriors sent from heaven
to bring prosperity to Earth.

Produce offspring, multiply, and radiate happiness.

Cultivate happiness. Foster happiness.

❧

Harmony exists for the sake of prosperity.

Cooperation exists for the sake of prosperity.

So work together, hand in hand,
for the sake of prosperity.

❧

Do not attempt to eliminate evil.

Do not attempt to eliminate discord.

Do not attempt to eliminate disharmony.

First ask yourself:

"Am I making an imprint of prosperity
as a child of God?"

"Am I manifesting prosperity in the way I live?"

Search for the answer in your heart.

Then make it come true.

That is how you can create a new era of great prosperity.

This verse characterizes the Shinto god Ameno Mina-kanushi's view on prosperity and evil. It starts with simple yet powerful words about the truth of prosperity. It would be fruitless to question its authenticity. Its truth is not about logic; it goes beyond reasoning. It simply leaves no room for debate, because it is stated with absolute certainty.

Then it offers a revolutionary, positive perspective. What seems like stagnation and decline is only a prelude to a prosperous future. Even when the curtain is drawn, it will rise again after the intermission.

This verse declares that it is a human responsibility to prosper. It is not about whether we want to be prosperous; it is simply our duty as human beings. It is an obligation we have to fulfill, like paying taxes. Prosperity is not a possibility, but a condition for being human. This is to say, if we do not achieve prosperity, we are going against God's Will. This firm stance that Ameno Minakanushi takes is an expression of his strong wish to help many people take a great leap to enter a higher realm of heaven. Even if we cannot achieve this instantaneously, we can get closer to it, as long as we keep thinking this way. Adopting this perspective is definitely an effective way to achieve prosperity.

THE START OF
A NEW LIFE

Start a new life as if you have been reborn.

Cast aside mistaken beliefs,
abandon mistaken ways of living,
and turn over a new leaf.

Enter a new phase in life.

As the water welling up from a spring is unstoppable,
so is the life force deep within our being.

It is impossible to suppress the energy
that rises up from deep within our being.

Feel this gushing power that keeps springing forth
without ever stopping.

Humans are endowed with this gushing power.

Use it to be born anew and start a new life.

The Shinto teaching of starting a new life is similar to Zen Buddhism's teaching of cutting off all ties with your past as if you've been born anew. This is one way of making a leap to enter the world of light.

The analogy of the spring is one of Ameno Mina-kanushi's favorite metaphors for describing our life energy. We cannot hold back the water that wells up from a spring. It may not seem to take much energy for water to well up from a spring, but it would take a lot of energy to hold that water back. Even if we tried to fill in the spring with concrete, the water would find its way out somewhere; it would emerge sooner or later. We all have a gushing power within like that of the groundwater.

Even when we think we have exhausted all our strength and it's all over, we still have energy deep within. Even if the water disappears from the surface, it keeps running underground as a subterranean stream. In the same way, spiritual energy runs throughout our bodies and wells up from the depths of our heart. We must be aware of this spring of energy inside us.

If you are in the midst of adversity and believe that you have used up all your strength, remember that inside you remains a reservoir of power that you can tap into. Remember that we all have infinite power within.

This verse tells us to live vigorously, like the waters of a spring. Even if we encounter obstacles on our way forward, we have the power within us to emerge from underneath in some way or other. When we see ourselves from this perspective, we can feel a strong sense of courage welling up inside us.

Our inner power is much stronger than we think. It is true that the more we train our soul, the stronger it becomes. But with or without training, the soul in its original state is extremely powerful. When we are born and start living in this material world, however, we begin to limit our ability by disbelieving our infinite potential and gradually locking ourselves into a limited world. But we were originally endowed with a much stronger spiritual energy.

Our life energy flows into us through a grand pipe connected to the source of our energy: God. Nothing can hold back this energy; it will emerge in some form or other. Knowing that this power exists inside us is a first step to living a life of courage.

A HEART
OF BEAUTY

We are beautiful as we are.

Beauty is about growing beautifully just as we are.

Beauty is about having an accepting heart.

Beauty is about living meekly,
with gratitude for the life God has given us.

Beauty is about accepting and fulfilling
the mission that God has entrusted to us.

This verse reminds us that human beings are beautiful just as we are. What brings out our innate beauty is a heart that accepts what is asked of us.

We often discuss what gives birth to evil and the ways we cloud or distort our hearts, but this may all be about whether we are being meek. We often create our own suffering by being defiant, creating distortions, or forcing ourselves to try to live a different kind of life. But all these issues can be solved the moment we start living meekly. If you look back over your own life and feel that your life hasn't been beautiful, ask yourself whether you have been living with an accepting heart.

We often run into problems and difficulties when we focus too much on our own self-improvement. At such times, take a moment to stop and ask yourself if you have a meek heart that accepts the Will of God as it is or a defiant heart that obscures your beauty. Remember, when you simply live with an accepting heart, you do not have to try to be beautiful, because you already are beautiful, just as you are.

FREEDOM OF THE SOUL

The soul is all and everything.

The soul has complete freedom to transform itself.

It can become so big that it looks down on Earth.

It can become so small that it looks up at an ant.

The soul is a formless energy.

It is a thinking energy.

It is an intellectual energy.

The soul can transform itself freely. Although you may understand this concept, you may still recognize yourself and others as physical beings with faces, arms, and legs, so it is probably difficult to imagine what it is like to be a soul. For example, I often talk about how each soul is made up of six different parts that take turns being born into this world. But you will probably have a hard time grasping this concept as long as you recognize yourself as a physical being.

When we experience at first hand the truth that the soul is a formless energy, we will gain a true understanding of the purpose of our life on Earth: that all of us are born into physical bodies to train and polish our souls. Many souls retain the shapes of their physical bodies even after they leave this world, because that's how they recognize themselves. But this is not their original state of being. They are taking these physical forms because they still haven't recognized the true state of their soul, which has complete freedom to transform itself.

This awareness of the soul leads us to a realization that the mind is what we really are. If I asked you whether you have a mind, you would probably answer, "Yes." But we cannot see the mind. It is invisible and does not take a physical form. Although we all know that we have a mind and that it governs our thoughts, it is invisible to our eyes. This formless existence is our true self. When we recognize ourselves as formless energy, we understand the true meaning of the phrase, "The soul is all and everything. The soul has a complete freedom to transform itself."

Life in this World Is Like a Movie

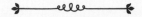

Suppose you are watching a movie in a movie theater. You see many scenes with different characters. Although you are only watching the images on the screen, you can get so absorbed that you feel as though they're real. You may feel as if you are actually there, inside the movie. This is how it feels when we see this world from the other world, the spirit world.

We experience many different things over the course of our life in this world. Sometimes we suffer from distress and sorrow, and at other times we feel joy and happiness. But when we end our life on Earth and return to the other world, we realize that our life in this world was like a play, and we understand that we were going through these experiences as part of our role in the play called life. Whatever the role we had—a king, a princess, a warlord, or a peasant—when the play is over, we all return backstage, where we even meet the characters that died in the middle of the play and have now come back to life.

Life in the physical world is like a movie or a play. Our experiences seem very real to us, but when we return to the other world, we learn that they have all been temporary.

THE MIND
AND ILLNESS

Human beings are originally perfect.

It is the imperfect image of the self
that you draw within the mind
that is manipulating how you see yourself,
that is causing your suffering.

Know that you are originally perfect,
that originally, illness does not exist,
that originally, you are healthy.

Why do only humans develop cancer and ulcers?

Why do only humans develop neuroses
and heart disease?

Have you seen a lion suffering from heart disease?

Have you seen a giraffe suffering from rheumatism?

Have you seen a fish suffering from the cold?

Human beings even create illnesses
for dogs and cats and hospitalize them.

Treating them with injections and medicines
is simply nonsense.

Cancer is one of the main causes of death.

It is not a virus that creates cancer.

It is our minds that create cancer.

Cancer is created by our self-punishing thoughts.

Cancer is a manifestation of
our desire for self-destruction.

❧

In this verse, the Shinto god Ameno Minakanushi says that illness originally does not exist. But we find all kinds of illnesses and disabilities in this world. Some people are sick and suffer from aches and pains. Others are blind, deaf, or crippled. But all physical symptoms and impediments disappear when we return to heaven. There are no sick people in heaven. Hell is the only place in the spirit world where we find pain and suffering.

Knowing this spiritual truth can help us gain a better understanding of this verse. The phrase, "originally, illness does not exist," means that illness does not exist in heaven. Heaven is a world created by God where no one suffers from sickness, pain, or disability. Although this verse was created based on the perspective from heaven, the same principle can be applied to our life in this world and can help us improve our physical well-being.

When you think about it, humans suffer from all kinds of ailments that other animals—fish, giraffes, and lions—do not. We humans develop such a wide variety of diseases that even medical students have a hard time learning them all. We even let our pets suffer from lifestyle diseases that are cured when they are set free in nature. Why do we complicate our lives by suffering from so many diseases? This shouldn't be how we live.

Those who are sick almost always suffer from mental discord. Illnesses are manifestations of mental conflicts. The weakest parts of our body are affected by our own disharmonious thoughts and become the seat of the disease. This is the process of developing an illness. Although it doesn't happen to everyone, miraculous healing of incurable cancer sometimes occurs when patients solve issues in their mind.

Humans have the power to build our own bodies. We have the ability to create our own appearance. We can also strengthen our body by training our muscles and legs. This is the positive aspect of our mind's influence over our body, but it can also have the negative effect of creating illness.

According to Ameno Minakanushi, illness is not transmitted from one person to another. Rather, a conflict in the mind manifests as illness. This is the truth of illness that we see when we look at it from a spiritual viewpoint. We are seeing an increase in the number of illnesses today because we are increasingly stressed and distressed by modern life.

Of course, the process of developing an illness can be complicated, and various factors have to come into play for the initial cause in the mind to manifest as a physical symptom. Whatever the elements that intervene in between, the main cause lies with the person who has sown the seeds of illness within.

As this verse suggests, all illnesses may just be manifestations of self-punishing thoughts. This may be especially true today: people are trying to escape from the stress of modern life, and this wish may have turned into a penance that causes illnesses. It is as if your body has gone on strike against too much stress.

We humans are blessed with the power to cure ourselves, which is why we can recover from sickness and injury. Our body will find a way to recover as long as it feels the need to do so. In some cases, even if we lose one bodily function, such as sight, another function, such as hearing, becomes stronger.

A lot of people wear glasses. But the fact that we are not born wearing glasses shows that we don't really need them. It may just be that our eyesight doesn't get better as long as we feel that we need glasses to see better.

I actually overuse my eyes; I probably use them a lot more than average. Knowing how intensively I use my eyes, you would probably expect me to have poor eyesight. But I do not wear glasses or contact lenses. In fact, I have 20/20 vision. Although I overuse my eyes, they're not going bad.

In fact, I have found a way to train my eyes so that they recover as soon as they start deteriorating. In the past, my eyesight has started to get worse several times, and I've had trouble reading signs at the train station—the words looked blurred and distorted. Whenever this has happened, I've said to myself, "I'll recover my eyesight within three days," and amazingly, I've been able to regain my eyesight within three days. You may find it difficult to believe, but it really is possible to heal your eyesight.

I didn't use any spiritual power to do this; I was able to do this even before I acquired the ability to commune with heaven. I just strongly believed that I could recover my eyesight. Even when I was much younger, I strained my eyes, and so I often found my sight deteriorating. But I couldn't afford to let my eyes go bad, since my work depended on them, so I decided that I would not wear glasses, even if my eyesight was going bad. As soon as I made this decision, I found my eyesight starting to improve. By refusing to wear glasses, I gave my eyes no option but to recover. My eyes recovered because it would simply be very inconvenient if they didn't.

The ciliary muscles that surround the optic lens control whether we can see objects that are far away or nearby. Our eyesight depends on how these muscles move, so you will be able to improve your eyesight if you can control these muscles. This is all we need to do to recover eyesight. But many people are unable to do this because they cannot take control of these muscles.

Humans are originally capable of healing ourselves. We can recover from illness if we earnestly wish to recover health. Based on my personal experience of recovering my eyesight by refusing to wear glasses, too, I am convinced that Ameno Minakanushi's claim that we have the power to heal illness is true.

THE MYSTERY
OF LIFE

What is the true essence of life? Ameno Minakanushi describes our existence by categorizing our being into different "bodies": physical bodies, astral bodies, spirit bodies, light bodies, divine light bodies, and divine bodies.

The spirit world is made up of different dimensions, and inhabitants of each dimension take different kinds of bodies. We reside in a physical body while living in this world of the third dimension, but in the Posthumous World of the fourth dimension, we take an astral body, which we will eventually cast off before we move on to a higher dimension. As we ascend to higher dimensions, the form we take changes from the astral body to the spirit body, the light body, the divine light body, and the divine body, which is a highly purified spiritual energy.

Although the astral body is a spiritual entity, it is still closely tied to the consciousness of the physical body, so it has coarse vibrations and a close affinity for the material world. We cast off our astral body as we move up to higher dimensions, but these astral bodies that we shed remain floating around in the Posthumous World. These floating, astral bodies resemble our physical bodies at first, but as time passes, they gradually disintegrate and lose their shape until they eventually become floating energies. When these energies combine with other thought energies, they transform into new astral beings.

Affected by various energies, the astral bodies reconstruct themselves, and in many cases, they become part of various existences in hell. Actually, the majority of the evil spirits in hell transform themselves by using the floating astral bodies.

I have seen this for myself, so I know it to be true: when these floating energies start taking shape, they coalesce into new creatures. People's negative thoughts can turn into frightening creatures when these energies dwell in the astral body, the spiritual mantle of the soul, which has a close affinity to the physical body. For example, if the energies of various people's jealousies coalesce, they start to take the shape of a monstrous creature like you would read about in a fairy tale. Many of these monstrous creatures exist in the Posthumous World of the fourth dimension of the spirit world. These are not original creations of God.

The majority of them were created by the combination of people's thought energies and floating astral bodies.

Which form the soul takes correlates with its level of spiritual awareness. The souls in astral bodies in the fourth dimension still cling to their material life on Earth, and they are yet to be fully purified.

The soul in a spirit body becomes more refined and acquires the ability to teleport. When the soul is in an astral body, it is still not fully capable of traveling from one place to another instantly. But once it becomes a spirit body, the soul gains more control and becomes able to manifest its will as action, which means that it becomes extremely easy for the soul in the spirit body to transport itself instantaneously. As a spirit body, the soul also gains the ability to change its appearance at will. It can use the power of its will to freely change what it is wearing from a Japanese kimono to a dress, for example.

When souls reach the sixth dimension, they take the form of light bodies. The light body is made of photons, so it shines brightly. When souls move up to the Bodhisattva World of the seventh dimension, they take divine light bodies.

Souls dwell in divine bodies once they reach the

Tathagata World of the eighth dimension. When spirits from the eighth dimension are born into this world, it is as if we are seeing God's Will manifesting on Earth. This is because the condition of becoming a tathagata is to live with the heart of God. Tathagatas serve as an artery of God's body, while the spirits of the ninth dimension are like the heart, pumping blood throughout the body.

Tathagatas of the eighth dimension and the Grand Tathagatas in the ninth dimensions no longer take human form. Spiritually, they act as arteries of spiritual energy and as the heart that pumps that energy, respectively. The ten Grand Spirits in the ninth dimension serve as ten hearts, each of which pumps blood that nourishes a different part of the body through the arteries that are the tathagatas in the eighth dimension. This energy then flows through the artery to spirits in the Bodhisattva World of the seventh dimension and the inhabitants of the World of Light in the sixth dimension, like blood flowing through the capillaries to the entire body. This is how God's energy provides nourishment throughout creation. Thus, the essence of the soul is a formless energy that changes its shape freely as it moves up to different levels of the spirit world.

The Multidimensional Structure of the Spirit World

Physics and mathematics have shown that, beyond the three-dimensional physical world we live in, there exist the worlds of the fourth, fifth, sixth, seventh, eighth, and ninth dimensions. But scientists haven't been able to offer clear descriptions of these worlds.

Through my spiritual investigation and research, I've gained an understanding of the different dimensions of the spirit world.

The fourth dimension is the world where people go immediately after death. It is known as the Posthumous World. The lower part of the fourth dimension is the place known as hell, while the upper reaches are known as the Astral Realm.

Above the fourth dimension is the World of Goodness in the fifth dimension. This is a world populated by good-hearted souls with a natural disposition toward goodness.

Above the World of Goodness is the World of Light of the sixth dimension. This is where divine spirits reside. People on Earth often worship the inhabitants of this world as saints and deities. The World of Light is also where leaders and experts in a variety of fields return after their death.

The world above the World of Light is the World of Bodhisattvas, or angels, in the seventh dimension. The main focus of the inhabitants of this world is helping others—performing acts of love. They have very few worries about themselves and are mainly concerned about how they can save the souls of as many people as possible and guide them to happiness. The spirits that reside in the World of Bodhisattvas in the seventh dimension are embodiments of love.

The World of Tathagatas of the eighth dimension is inhabited by the souls of great historical figures who shaped the civilizations of each era. They include religious leaders and philosophers, as well as political leaders.

The ninth dimension is the Cosmic World or the world of Earth's highest divinities. This is also known as the World of Saviors, where Grand Spirits, including Shakyamuni Buddha, Jesus Christ, and Moses, reside. The inhabitants of this world come down to Earth once every few thousand years to teach fundamental philosophies and teachings to establish the very principles that give rise to great civilizations.

For more information about the multidimensional structure of the spirit world, please refer to two of my other publications: *The Laws of the Sun* [New York: IRH Press, 2013] and *The Nine Dimensions* [New York: IRH Press, 2012].

THE SHINTO GODS

The teachings of the Truths
must be brought into politics.

It may be very well to put an end to the Imperial system,
but a new system must be established to replace it.

It is noteworthy that Ameno Minakanushi feels this way about the imperial system. This is his challenge to the current system, and it represents his strong wish to establish a system of governance that reflects God's Will.

The philosophy of Shintoism is very well-organized and is based on theocracy. Historically, the Shinto gods have guided Japan's emperors in leading the country. It is because of this divine guidance that Japan's Imperial system has survived for more than two thousand years. However, a question remains as to whether this is an all-encompassing system.

If we study the history of the Japanese Imperial system, we see that it serves the role of maintaining balance by preserving the principle of order. Japan once had a dual power structure in which power was divided between the feudal government of the Shogunates and the emperor. While the emperor always remained at the top, the government officials underneath were frequently replaced. This system continued for a long time, and I think that the Shinto gods intended to keep it that way.

What we are searching for now, however, is not a symbolic system, but a new social structure in which enlightened, highly virtuous teachers of the Truths stand at the pinnacle of a new world order. The deities and divine spirits of other religions seem to be in agreement with the Shinto gods in this respect.

Japan, the Nation with the Longest History Under a Single Dynasty

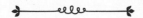

Kojiki (Records of Ancient Matters), a sacred Shinto text compiled in 712, mentions the Primordial Seven, the seven generations of deities preceding Emperor Jimmu, Japan's first emperor and the founder of the imperial dynasty. These records show that Japan has been governed by a unified dynasty for 2,700 years and has an even longer history that includes the era of the Primordial Seven. In fact, Japan is the nation with the longest history under a single dynasty.

Although Greek civilization flourished, its dynasty eventually went to ruin. Rome was once known as the Eternal City, but it only lasted for about a thousand years before the fall of the Roman Empire. China claims to have five thousand years of history, but it has been governed by many dynasties, even within the last two or three thousand years. China wasn't always governed by the Han Chinese. Non-Chinese ethnics inside and around China, such as Mongolians and Manchurians, have governed the country at different times. So although China has a long history, it hasn't been ruled by a single dynasty. In contrast, Japan has been ruled by emperors of a single dynasty for the last 2,700 years, and this is a miraculous achievement worth celebrating. In this respect, I believe that Japan should be designated a world heritage nation.

A CRITICISM OF DEMOCRACY

The fourth dimension has
the largest population in the spirit world.

The population decreases
as we move up to higher dimensions,
through the fifth, sixth, and above.

The higher their spiritual awareness becomes,
the fewer their numbers become.

❧

Look at the democratic system on Earth
based on this structure of the spirit world.

You will see that rule of the majority leads to
rule by the fourth-dimensional principles.

This criticism of democracy is compelling. The source of confusion on Earth today is the predominance of the principles of the fourth dimension. Democracy, or majority rule, lets those with a lower level of consciousness have greater say because they outnumber those from higher worlds of heaven. This is one point of view we need to be aware of when thinking about our political system. Based on this spiritual Truth, I believe that the question of whether democracy is the best form of government deserves further consideration and discussion.

The Fundamental Basis of Politics

In democratic governance, it is essential that we make decisions based on our good conscience, which we can cultivate by trying to see things from the perspective of God. We need to always keep in mind what His Will was when he first implemented the system of governance in this world.

God has entrusted humans with the authority to govern this world because it was His Will that humans build the Kingdom of God, or heaven in this world. In the beginning, deities descended to this world to govern and guide human beings, but later on, the authority to govern the world, under normal circumstances, was given to human beings. But at turning points of history, when a nation faces crisis, God sends divine spirits to help people bring about revolutionary changes to start a new era. This is the idea that lies at the basis of politics. Thus, it is a fundamental mistake to think that the laws that human beings have created are almighty and that they rule the world. That would be like saying that the laws that physicists have created govern the universe. In understanding politics, we have to know that the mere thoughts and ideas that humans come up with do not change the fundamental rules and laws that God created to govern this world.

THE WORKINGS OF DESTINY

If our destiny were preordained,
even before we were born into this world,
it would not be possible to
take responsibility for our own life.

If our life path were fixed, and
the world we return to in the next world predestined,

our freedom to make our own choices and decisions
in our life on Earth would be greatly hampered.

❧

Our destiny is not preordained, because we are responsible for the choices and decisions we make in life. It would be an unjust world if we had to take responsibility for a life we didn't choose. Our world is subject to the principle of self-responsibility: each person is accountable for his or her own thoughts and actions, and this guarantees us the freedoms of thought, choice, and decision. Without these freedoms, we would be living like puppets, only to be cremated and displayed on a shelf after ending our life in this world. This would truly be an absurd view on life.

Hearing this, you may ask, "If we are so uncertain about the future of our lives and the world, then what roles do prophecy and foreknowledge play? How is it possible that some people know or see things before they happen?" Answering these questions is difficult because it's hard to fully understand how destiny works without the deep wisdom that comes from spiritual knowledge and experience.

Ameno Minakanushi explains the workings of destiny using the metaphor of a boat travelling down a river. A prophet is like a veteran boatman who knows every twist and turn of the river called life. He can tell the curve the boat will pass through an hour after it leaves and at what points the boat will pass through shoals and rapids, because he's travelled the river many times and knows the course of the river very well. But those travelling the river for the first time will find it amazing that the boat takes the exact course that the veteran boatman predicts.

Still, the speed of the boat will depend on the person rowing it. If that person is unskilled, the boat may run aground somewhere or he may stop the boat and get off. It is possible to predict the dangers that lie ahead to a certain extent if you know the course the boat will take—if you know, for example, where the rapids are and where the falls are. But you won't know whether you will be able to overcome these dangers until you actually take the ride. Similarly, certain elements come into play that change the course of our lives.

This is how destiny works. This is why some prophecies do not come to pass. Although I don't have the exact statistics, I estimate that more than 50 percent of people today end up in hell. But I doubt that they made a plan to go to hell before they were born into this world. They may have thought of the possibility, but I think it was unlikely that they actually planned it that way. But as people go down the river called life, some of their boats capsize, and some people drown. The trip may start out smoothly, but many people face dangers along the way, and some sink before they reach their destination. Those whose boats sink were probably aware of the dangers they would face, but they decided to take the ride anyway, because they believed that they would be safe. This is how life looks like from the spiritual perspective. We are not doing this for entertainment; we are in this for real.

THE DISCOVERY OF GOODNESS

Venture forth with a strong conviction
that there is no adversity.

When you pioneer a new path, you will come to know
that all that seemed like difficulties
were merely illusions.

The large cliff that stands before you to block your way
is just an illusion.

It is as ephemeral as the simmering of heat waves
or fog over the river.

Discover goodness in all things.

Discover goodness in all people.

Believe that only goodness exists in the world.

Believe that true goodness creates the world.

Believe that there is no pain or suffering
in the world created by goodness.

This verse speaks of the two important factors we need to ride out the river of destiny: self-awareness and self-determination.

Believing that all the people you meet in life have come to you to offer their blessings can actually make the world a better place. If you think evil of others, then you will be confronted with evil people. I am sure that many people know this to be true from experience. If you keep telling people how evil they are, they will start acting like evil people. We have to consider both the positive and negative sides of people, but I still believe that it will do us all good if we try to focus on the good and disregard the bad.

AN INDOMITABLE SPIRIT

When you try to spread these spiritual messages,
some may deny them,
and some may try to hinder your efforts.

Others may become jealous of the miraculous words.

Never mind their slander.

Never let their words intimidate or daunt you.

Ask your heart what to do.

If your heart tells you that this is the right thing to do,
that this accords with God's Will,
cast out all evil arising from the physical world.

Carry out the mission of publishing these words.

Force through the mission of disseminating these words.

❧

Do not hesitate.

Do not give in to the conventional view.

Do not yield to public opinion.

There are times when we must carry out our mission
at all costs.

❧

This verse talks about indomitable resolve and decisive
action as the elements essential to successful travel down
the river of destiny. Taking decisive action is in fact the
final key to a life of triumph.

These are words of encouragement for those who
are trying to spread the spiritual Truths. Those who are
enthusiastic about sharing the Truths are often ridiculed
and criticized. But at such times, knowing that we have
heaven's support fills us with courage.

ACTS OF LOVE

One thing is clear:
what you do for the sake of others
will never, ever work against you.

In this world,
you may sometimes be misunderstood or insulted
for the good you try to do for others.

You may suffer the pain of not being understood,
of having your actions completely misinterpreted.

But never be a consequentialist.

Even if your acts of love did not bear fruit
this in no way means that you have failed.

Your acts of love, your thoughts of love,
will never, ever be in vain.

❧

Our thoughts become reality in the other world. In this world, however, our thoughts may not always produce the outcome we want. We may even end up in a disadvantageous position. But even if we are misunderstood or have not achieved the outcome we hoped for, in the eyes of God, the actions we've taken with a sincere wish to benefit others will be as real and successful as can be. I believe this to be true.

THE POWER OF PERSEVERANCE

The biggest difference between
human beings and animals is that humans
have the power to embrace ideals.

This power is what separates us from the animals.

So never lose sight of your ideals.

Take action with a strong resolve
to achieve what you aspire to.

And make endeavors to this end.

Creating Your Own Destiny

Making an effort should not be a drudgery.

It should be a joy.

Perseverance is the most important element in achieving success. We can't achieve success without perseverance. With the power of faith, sometimes things go exactly the way we want them to, but this ideal state is unlikely to last for an entire lifetime. There will be times when we get involved in trouble and other times when we face disappointment. No matter what happens, what is required of us is the virtue of perseverance. Perseverance is what will save us and lead us to success in the end.

The idea that the virtue of perseverance and forbearance is the key to success is taught not only by Shintoism, but by Buddhism as well. We lose sight of the purpose of life when we start thinking that all that matters is the result, that we will be happy if we achieve what we want and unhappy if we don't. If that were all there is to life, there would be no point in going through spiritual training in this world.

When you have achieved success, aim for even greater success while humbly and carefully making continuous efforts. When you fail, pioneer a new path to success by learning from the failure and calmly persevering. Living with this attitude is essential to making your hopes come true.

A LEAP OF THE SOUL

Believe in yourself as a child of God.

Believe in others as children of God.

Moving your boat forward while encountering
no evil, no harm, and no storms
is what makes an ordinary life.

This way of life should not be your goal.

When you embrace ideals and live up to them,
you can no longer live an ordinary life.

You will start living an out-of-the-ordinary life.

❧

Life is a succession of opportunities.

Life is a succession of leaps forward.

❧

Look at that vaulting box.

Woe on those who see it as an obstacle.

It's not an obstacle.

Because by leaping across it,
you experience a sense of exhilaration,
achievement, and accomplishment.

Hardships are like vaulting boxes
placed in your path to strengthen your soul.

Imagine yourself becoming a giant like Gulliver.

Stones and spears thrown at you can no longer harm you.

Because you think of yourself as a human being,
you believe that the spears that others throw at you
have the power to kill you.

But if you think of yourself as a giant,
the spears become as harmless as mosquito bites.

You don't believe that you will die of a mosquito bite.

This verse serves as an important piece of advice for us all. It encourages us not to fear criticism and to spread far and wide what we believe to be the Truths. We are to carry out our mission in life undaunted. I hope that we can together spread the Truths all over the world, with these words as the source of our courage.

Chapter Five

DISCOVERING
NEW
HORIZONS
of SUCCESS

DISCOVERING ETERNAL LIFE

Some time ago, a design expo was held in a city in Japan. I had sensed, even before this event, that the citizens wished to create a culture of their own and develop cultural interests. And I believe that their strong wish led them to hold the design exposition. But this made me contemplate the ephemerality of designing external forms. Outer appearances will eventually fade, but the design of the human heart will never decline. Once formed, our eternal, imperishable life will never disappear.

Fact is fact, and truth is truth. The fact that human beings have eternal life is unchangeable and cannot be disproven by anyone. I, on the other hand, have been providing evidence to prove this Truth through the numerous books I have published. I have written each of my books on the sole premise that humans have eternal life and that our souls are in a process of eternal evolution. I have published all my books to reveal this basic Truth.

Some of my readers may have read many of my other books, and for some, this may be the first one they've picked up. Others may have been dubious about the authenticity of my work when they started reading it. Regardless of what triggered you to pick up this book, if you can find in my words even a germ of truth that resonates with your soul, this is the truth I would like you to believe: *Humans have eternal life. Humans were bestowed with eternal life at the time of creation.* This is an undeniable truth. It is an indisputable fact.

So in this chapter, entitled "Discovering New Horizons of Success," I would like to begin my discussion with a contemplation on the individual lives that exist within the flow of the great river of eternal life, because this perspective is essential to the definition of success.

Achieving worldly recognition and aiming to perfect a life of sixty or seventy years in this world is not true success. True success should be eternal, just as human life is eternal. Any philosophy of success without this premise of the eternity of our life would easily collapse.

Eventually, we will all leave this world, but our life will continue even after we die. We have everlasting life. Christianity teaches that those who do good and believe in the Lord Jesus Christ will gain eternal life and that those who do not shall wither like grass and fade like the flowers on the field. But our life is not evanescent like that of grass and flowers on the field. If you could recall the memories that lie deep within your soul, you would find that you have been born in various parts of the world in different eras. I have been trying to prove this by publishing spiritual messages from the great figures in history who now reside in heaven. If these souls ceased to exist when their lives on Earth ended, it would have been impossible to deliver their words in the form of spiritual messages. The publication of their words proves their existence. All humans and all life are equally valuable. All are blessed with eternal life. They manifest themselves differently by their thoughts, will, and actions. The consequences of our thoughts and behavior not only come to fruition in this world, but also determine the kind of life we will lead in the afterworld.

The kind of success that I would like to talk about in this chapter is not the superficial, conspicuous, or self-satisfying form of success that you can read about in many other books. With this basic Truth of the eternal nature of human life as my premise, I would like to discuss three levels of success: the personal level, the corporate level, and the national level.

BEARING THE FRUIT OF ENLIGHTENMENT

What is personal success? This is something that many of us wonder at some point in life. The meaning of the word *success* is probably very close to what we refer to as *happiness*. From the standpoint of an eternal life, success is identical to the true happiness that we teach at my organization, Happy Science. So what is this success that goes hand in hand with happiness? There are three basic conditions for true success.

The first condition for success, in simple terms, is to live your life as such that other people appreciate your being there. They may or may not actually express their feelings, but your life is a success if people around you feel glad to have shared with you some of the few moments that they have in this life and this era, here and now.

To put it the other way around, the last thing you want is for people around you to say that life would have been better without you. This would basically be the same as being told that your life on Earth has been completely worthless and that it would be better if you could airbrush out your entire life.

How should we live so that others will appreciate our presence? The answer to this question brings us to the second condition for success, which is more proactive than the first condition. It is to leave behind achievements of your undertaking, footprints of your efforts, or monuments to your accomplishments. These should be things that not only you recognize, but that other people acknowledge as well.

If you have a career, you can make achievements through your work. If you are a full-time homemaker, your achievements can be measured by the looks on the faces of your family. The happy faces of your children, your spouse, and your parents are the signs of your accomplishments. Whatever the form may be, the second condition for success is to leave behind traces of your life that others can recognize as positive.

The third condition for success is to create your own philosophy through the life you live. Of course, most people will not be able to leave behind a philosophy that could be published as a book. But it doesn't have to be something difficult or something that others study. The philosophy of your life should be created based on the lessons you've learned from your own life. It should be something that you feel is worth sharing with others. It is your discovery that you've made over the course of the several decades of your life and that you can pass on to future generations.

This may sound easy, but you'll see that it's not when you ask yourself what your philosophy is. What would you say if you were told to stand up and share your personal philosophy now? What are some lessons you have learned from life, and what are some discoveries that you can call your own? Can you expound on them clearly and precisely in a way that will be helpful to others?

Philosophy is not something that springs out of nowhere one day. It is something that you can acquire through the process of careful study, consideration, and practice. Only the important lessons that you've learned from experience develop into a philosophy. Each of us can and should develop our own philosophy of life, because a philosophy of our own is proof of the spiritual progress we have made in this lifetime.

Just as our physical appearances vary, the levels of enlightenment we can achieve vary depending on the person. But as an individual with a name and a unique personality, it is important that you develop your original philosophy, even if you feel that it is inferior to that of others, because when you refine it, this original philosophy of yours will eventually become your own enlightenment.

Imprint your philosophy in your mind, and use it as wisdom to teach, help, and guide others through the course of your life. God gave us this vast third-dimensional space for us to share with the other seven billion people alive today because He expects us to gain precious experiences through our journey on this spaceship called Earth. These experiences should not only include personal ones that we feel complacent about. We should instead share our experiences with others so that they can learn from our experiences, too.

Even if you do not express your philosophy in a concrete form while you are alive, you can share the wisdom you have gained when you returned to the other world—the spirit world. The divine messages that numerous heavenly spirits have been bringing to this world through me are not rigid and adamant like bricks, cement, or concrete blocks. Their words are pearls of wisdom that they have polished with their experiences. Through their words of light, they are casting upon us the spiritual awakening that they have acquired.

The success of each individual's life should carry the ring, substance, elegance, and aroma of their enlightenment. Enlightenment may not be something that we can pick up and show to others, but we can still sense the unique scent of the individual's soul, just as every fruit and flower gives its own scent. We can definitely distinguish the smell of the peaches as we pass underneath a peach tree and the cherry blossoms as we pass by a cherry tree. In the same way, the soul of each person emits its fragrance, its own rich and aromatic scent of enlightenment throughout the person's life. The fragrance of each person's enlightenment leaves us with telling effects, a distinctive resonance, and special circumstances as we come across one another.

It is actually the collective, synthesized scents of each individual's enlightenment that create the atmosphere of the world. If that atmosphere has an unpleasant, rotten, foul smell, this world will become a dark, gloomy, bleak, and nasty place in which we find it difficult to live. On the contrary, we can easily imagine how wonderful this world will become when it is filled with the pleasant, heavenly fragrance of enlightenment.

These three conditions for success based on the

enlightenment of each individual serve as the foundation of my philosophy of success. The first condition is to become someone that everybody feels grateful is there, instead of becoming a nuisance that everyone dislikes. The second condition is to leave behind a concrete achievement that others can recognize so that it is clear to everyone what you've accomplished during your lifetime.

The third condition is to imprint the lessons you've learned in your heart and develop them into your own philosophy. As you further refine and improve your philosophy, you will be able to make it your spiritual awakening, which will bear the fruits and flowers of enlightenment.

It is my earnest wish that you will understand and apply this fundamental view to your life so that you can achieve personal success.

CULTIVATING THE VIRTUE OF LEADERSHIP

Next, I would like to apply this philosophy of success to the corporate or organizational level and consider the type of success we should pursue.

When we look at the world, it may seem as though thriving businesses and successful firms are the signs of human prosperity. Although the corporate system works well in modern society, we often lose sight of its heart. But what is the heart of corporations? Perhaps we can call it *the spirit* or *the mind* of a corporation, which is represented by the mission or purpose of the business.

The company's mission statement or credo states the business's objective. When new employees join a company, they usually learn during the orientation that the company's objective is to pursue profits. I am not saying that making money is bad. I believe that money can be a powerful tool that we can use for the betterment of the world. While there is not anything wrong with making profits in and of itself, what matters is the business's purpose. For what goals is the business pursuing profits? What is its ultimate aim? What are the thoughts or motives behind the company's pursuit of profits?

One thing we should keep in mind is that profits or returns are of neutral value. They can be good or bad, depending on how they are used. The thoughts or motives of the person who uses the profits and the end results the profits bring determine whether the profits are good or bad.

From a spiritual perspective, money used for a good cause is a gain, while money used for an evil cause is a loss. So even if your business is in the black based on the figures in your bank account, it may have plunged into the red spiritually.

Profits that are used to improve the world or create a better world appear in gold on its spiritual balance sheet and income statement, and money used to cause harm appears in red, black, or grey. The outward prosperity of a business that brings confusion to people's lives, destroys the environment, or lays waste to the hearts of the people is not worth more than withered grass on a riverbank. Without considering this perspective, it's hard to know whether you are bringing growth and prosperity to your company in the truest sense.

What, then, is the key to corporate success? It is the mindset of those who lead the company. Understanding of the mind or the inner world is an absolute prerequisite to becoming a leader. You need more than just the ability to hold a managerial position. Of course, doing your job correctly is, in itself, a form of love for others. You can use your skills to contribute to many different communities. But if you do your job simply for your own personal gain, to receive praise and rewards, or to benefit yourself only, you don't have a leader's heart. For this reason, I urge those in management who have never trained their mind to consider stepping down from their position immediately.

One of the requirements for becoming a leader, and the element that increases the caliber of a person's leadership, is virtue. The word *virtue* may have a rather old-fashioned ring to it, and people today may find it difficult to understand what it really means. But there are virtuous people, and what makes them virtuous is that they've spent far more time thinking of the happiness of others than they spend thinking of their own happiness.

Now, take a few moments to look within. Look back on the thoughts you've had during the past few decades of your life. Have most of them been about yourself or others? Or, if that's too long a period to recall, consider what kinds of thoughts you've had in the previous twenty-four hours or during the sixteen hours that you've been awake. What kinds of thoughts have occupied your mind? Have most of them been about yourself or others?

If your mind has been filled with thoughts about others, check to see whether they were positive or negative thoughts. Negative thoughts, such as insults, complaints, criticisms, and dissatisfaction with others or your environment will only make you virtueless.

Although we cannot see the thoughts that others hold in their minds while we live in this world, when we return to the other world, we will be able to see other people's thoughts clearly, as if we are looking through a glass window. The thoughts that we continue to hold in our mind will be gauged by the amount of light our souls emit in the other world. This is how virtue manifests itself.

Virtue remains invisible while it is sealed inside the physical body, but virtue leaks out in the same way that light leaks out through a crack. Imagine a ray of light leaking out of a silkworm's cocoon. That is what virtue is like.

Virtue is not something that we can pick up and show

for everyone to see, but the gauge of virtue is the amount of time that we have spent harboring thoughts of love toward others and thinking of others' happiness without considering our own benefit, without wishing for fame, and without defending our own interests.

Virtuous people are those who continue to harbor love for others. The total amount of time you spend thinking about others—thinking nurturing thoughts, forgiving thoughts, and caring thoughts—becomes your virtue. This is probably the simplest possible explanation of virtue; I think anyone can understand it.

Virtue is akin to love. The virtuous are the ones that fill their hearts with love. The process of creating virtue is similar to the way an oyster forms a pearl. Pearls grow within oysters in the same way that love grows in developmental stages, as I described in my book *The Laws of the Sun*.

A wish to offer your love to others is essential to becoming a virtuous person. Love should not be a give-and-take deal. It is a feeling of wanting to give without expecting anything in return. This is what I call *fundamental love*. The next level of love that those who have developed their capabilities and skills can practice is *spiritually nurturing love.* This is the love of leaders; it is a love that guides and teaches others. Many leaders practice this level of love.

The third level of love, above spiritually nurturing love, is *forgiving love*, which is a more difficult love to practice. Those who can practice spiritually nurturing love have acquired high levels of knowledge and skills, and thus they can recognize both the strengths and shortcomings of others. It is because they become keenly aware of people's abilities that they also start noticing people's faults. This is an issue many executives run into. While practicing spiritually nurturing love, they start focusing on other people's faults, mistakes, or shortcomings. Some of them become coldhearted and start treating others like tools or machines that serve and protect the organization or the company they manage, like how the state treated its people in Niccolo Machiavelli's *The Prince.*

Forgiving love helps us overcome this issue and raises us to a higher stage. Forgiving love is a heart of tenderness. It is an angelic love that forgives any mistakes and faults and embraces others as children of God. Forgiving love is a state of love that sees people from a religious standpoint.

An even higher state of love is *love incarnate*, which is a love of the giants of history who became the spirit of their age. These people's very lives are gospels to the people of their era. These great figures have been present in every region, in every period. Their love is not directed to a particular person but radiates out in all directions, shining brilliantly. People who are love incarnate light up the world like the light bulb that Thomas Edison invented.

Virtue grows in the same way that love develops: in stages. The only difference between the two is that love expresses itself through action, while virtue is part of our being. Love is a function that manifests itself as action. Love appears through our activities. Love is a relationship; it exists between people. It is a tangible manifestation of our thoughts.

Virtue, on the other hand, is not a function, action, or activity, but rather existence itself. We can't put all our virtue to use. Virtue is the wisdom accumulated within our soul. Virtue is a pearl of love, a crystallization of loving thoughts.

Virtue is like a crystal ball: although we can touch the outer surface of a crystal ball, we cannot touch its inner surface. We can see through to its center, but we cannot reach inside. Likewise, virtue is visible to anyone who wishes to see it, but we can never touch or grasp it with our hands.

FULFILLING THE MISSION OF HEAVEN THROUGH POLITICS

Selecting Virtuous Politicians and Revolutionizing the Government

We need virtuous leaders not only for corporate success, but also for national success. When a country faces a turning point and its people are lost about how to move forward, they shouldn't depend solely on their earthly intelligence to find the answers, nor follow the examples of other countries. They should seek divine guidance and try to find answers by asking for God's Will.

"How does our nation look through the eyes of God? What direction should politics move toward?" This is a matter of serious debate. This is what the political parties should be debating instead of vying for the number of votes they can win or the number of seats they can hold.

There are countless talks about problems in politics, including corruption, but what they all boil down to is that political leaders are virtueless. It is because of their lack of virtue that they cannot see the direction God wants us to aim for and thus don't know what path the country should take. Politicians are striving to find the right direction in their own way, which only makes them look greedy, egotistic, competitive, and self-centered in the public's view. If only they had virtue and could see the direction in which God wants to lead them, their efforts would bear fruit and be evaluated fairly. It is because they lack virtue that the people think that politicians only act out of self-preservation, for profit, or in their own interests. These assumptions may not be accurate, but that's how politicians appear to others because they have simply lost sight of their foundation; they have lost sight of their guiding star.

The world is now approaching a great turning point. It will undergo changes that will affect the future, and there will be much commotion and confusion. But there is a way out of the current confusion, and that is to return the affairs of state to the hands of those who originally handled them. That is to say, restore the order of heaven and fulfill the mission of heaven through politics. This is the only path to take, although there are various approaches we can take to achieve this goal.

For instance, the current government system in Japan, which consists of the Upper House and the Lower House, no longer functions efficiently. In particular, the Upper House is not fulfilling its role as a legislative conscience. It's supposed to be composed of people with good hearts and intelligence who act as a safeguard when the policies of government start to move in the wrong direction. But today, it doesn't seem to represent a gathering of people of good conscience, and it no longer carries out its original function either. I believe this system only makes the legislative process redundant, slowing down political functioning and causing inefficiency.

Many people today think that the current system, in which we use elections to select the government, is the only right kind of democracy—but they are wrong. Although this system helps prevent the worst kind of governance and raise the average level of politics, it is not necessarily the best form of government. In fact, the ideal form of politics has never been achieved through election-based democracy.

The reason for this is that the goal of selecting virtuous

people clashes with the process of competing based on personal gains and interests. Rivalry between candidates for election does not help us elect the virtuous.

The virtuous should be chosen and rise to the top naturally, without struggling to win votes by luring people with promises of profits and gains. They should not be torn into pieces and shaken up through the process of election.

The current election system doesn't allow the virtuous to be selected. The reasons for this may be obvious. But one of them is that it costs a great deal of money to run for office. Another reason is that politics is a very unstable job. And even if virtuous people get elected, they may find their colleagues' ethics too shallow to bear. There may be a number of other factors in the current system that work against selecting the virtuous. But now, we must take courage and revolutionize this system so that suitable people are chosen naturally.

There are several ways that we can go about achieving this revolution. One way I would like to propose is to split the Lower House into three groups. For instance, if we have six hundred representatives in the Lower House, one group comprising two hundred people should be trained as political experts. Under the current system, politicians get busy with election campaigns every two, three, or four years, which prevents them from concentrating on leading the national government.

The flood of information that surrounds us today requires experts who can handle specific issues in each field. Politicians who are elected every few years can't take the time to acquire the expertise necessary to manage the bureaucracy or to develop the ability to lead discussions with the top leaders of other countries to favorable outcomes. If we wish to make great accomplishments as a nation, we need politicians who are experts in their fields. At least one-third of the politicians, or about two hundred people, should be trained as political experts.

To become experts, new graduates don't necessarily have to pass a qualification exam at the time of graduation. Instead, I think they should have at least five years of experience in the field before taking a qualification examination to be eligible. This exam should include specialist knowledge in politics, economics, and law. But limiting it only to these areas would be no different from the current system of selecting bureaucrats.

What I would like to propose is that we choose people who have studied the teachings of the Truths and train them as political professionals. I think it is essential that we choose people who have expertise in their own fields and who have gained a deep understanding of spirituality and the world of Truth.

If anyone fears of the possibility of choosing eccentric people through this process, then we can hold a national review every ten years, like how we review Supreme Court justices in Japan. If they manage to pass every review, then they should be allowed to remain at their posts until retirement age. It is essential that we have politicians with long-term tenure and with expertise and an understanding of spiritual Truths to lead the country.

Another one-third of the six hundred representatives, or the second group of politicians, should consist of functional or occupational representatives and take over the duties of the Upper House. We can perhaps call this system an industrial democracy.

Each industry has associations and societies that represent it. For instance, bankers belong to the Bankers Association, and executive officers of hometown banks take turn serving as the association's chair. Politicians in the second group should be selected from the top leaders of every industry, including steel, engineering, and oil. The representatives should be elected by vote to take part in government for a period of four years. They should leave their posts after a single term of four years so that new leaders in each industry have an opportunity to take part in politics. This system will replace the Upper House.

Those who are selected as industry representatives should be free to support whatever party they choose to belong to and to engage in whatever kinds of activities they like during their four-year term. This will prevent them from being pressured to act on behalf of special-interest lobbyists.

The remaining one-third—the final two hundred representatives—should be chosen by election. One hundred representatives should be chosen in a national election, and the remaining one hundred should be selected in regional elections in which an average of two representatives are chosen from each state.

To sum up, I propose that the government consist of three groups: one group of expert politicians, one group of industry representatives, and one group of elected officials. The expert politicians will be able to prevent political crises; the industry representatives will bring sophisticated skills and knowledge to the government, and the elected officials will bring new blood into politics. Each of these groups could then select one candidate to run for the post of the head of state, who should be chosen by national referendum. I believe this system will allow us to choose the most suitable person to be the top national leader and that this government system will greatly improve politics.

Implementing a New Tax System and Beneficial Administrative Services

Another issue that requires reconsideration is the current tax system. From a divine perspective, no more than 10 percent of earnings should be taken in taxes, whether from individuals or corporations. This is the long-held view of heaven on the tax system.

Today, some people pay more than 50 percent of their earnings in taxes, and corporations are burdened with heavy taxes as well. This high tax rate is causing the high-income class to lose motivation to work, while corporations create various jobs as tax-saving measures, which prevents them from focusing on developing their core business. This is simply unproductive.

The total tax rate should not be more than 10 percent. These taxes should be the total national revenue—the budget that the government can use to run the country. This budget should then be allocated to each of the ministry offices or government departments.

If the ministries need more money than has been allocated for them, they should be allowed to offer services for which they can charge fees and use those for additional activities. If they want to increase their budget, all they have to do is offer services that create revenue. This system will allow government offices to adopt business principles.

The current system includes numerous unnecessary government services. According to business principles, everything unnecessary will be eliminated. Services that the people don't find economically valuable will be terminated. Services that the people find useful will generate revenue. If each of the government ministries reevaluates its services thoroughly and starts offering services that benefit the people, they will all be able to earn additional income, giving them the budget for any additional activities they might like to engage in.

We should also reform the budget system. Under the current system in Japan, each ministry basically has to use its entire budget during the fiscal year or in the following year. But no organization uses all its budget in a single year. Obviously, it would be impossible to run a household or business that way. Every household needs to save money for children's school tuition and emergencies such as unexpected hospitalization. Businesses need to brace themselves for recession. That's why they set aside internal reserves; it's only natural that they save a certain percentage of their profits.

As strange as it may appear, however, the Japanese government uses up the entire budget every year, because otherwise the government would not be able to create a fiscal plan or budget for the next year. We see a rash of road construction work toward the end of the fiscal year as a result, but this is a truly ridiculous situation that should not be tolerated.

Each ministry can take an independent accounting system or have the Finance Ministry allocate budget for them. In any case, what's important is for every ministry to create a long-term budget so that they can use accumulated savings on major projects or on investments every five or ten years.

There are also some government departments that I feel can be cut down. Ministries other than the Ministry of Foreign Affairs, the Ministry of Economy, Trade, and Industry, the Ministry of Finance, and the Ministry of Internal Affairs and Communication can be scaled down to agencies or small offices. They don't necessarily have to remain ministries. That way, we can save a lot of tax money.

Government agencies can sometimes help support

certain industries. For example, Japan's banking industry received administrative guidance from the Finance Ministry after the Second World War, and this guidance furthered the development of Japanese banks. But financial deregulation and free competition are necessary to foster the industry's growth. This may cause financial instability, but just like any other industry, the banking industry needs to rationalize its operations so that we can find ways to waste less time, effort, and money. Government protection can help the banking industry under special circumstances, but such protection is generally unnecessary.

There are many ways to prevent the waste of taxpayer's money, and the government should not be allowed to raise taxes without making an effort to reduce them. The maximum tax rate should be 10 percent. If the government needs additional revenue, it should earn it by selling its services. The government should run the country within its budget, just as individuals should try to live within their means and set aside a percentage of their earnings for savings. In the same way that we accumulate virtue, so can we strengthen the economic power of the country, leading it to further development.

PURSUING PERSONAL HAPPINESS AND PUBLIC HAPPINESS

My dream is to create an ideal world, a world of Truth, and this should be about not only our spirituality, but also the physical world.

How do you know if your town, country, or world is becoming a better place to live? You can tell if you and the people around you are becoming happier every year. If a nation is on a path to becoming a first-class country in the truest sense, then feelings of its people should be increasingly happy. The value of spiritual Truths should be recognized in the fields of economics and politics so as to increase happiness among the people.

Now is the time for us to stand up and take action to realize happiness in this world. We shouldn't remain silent. We shouldn't remain quiet. Asking questions is important to bringing about improvements to this world. If we see anything that we feel is wrong, we should bring it to the attention of others. We should not complain or criticize for the sake of complaining or criticizing. We need to speak up, because we need to create a righteous world, an ideal world on Earth.

To create an ideal world of happiness, each of us needs to pursue two objectives in our daily life. The first objective is to pursue personal happiness. This is not about pursuing your egotistical desires. The pursuit of personal happiness is about seeking enlightenment—the happiness that accompanies spiritual awakening. It is about experiencing the happiness of watching the world develop around you from an enlightened perspective. The pursuit of personal happiness entails a way of life that increases our happiness while we maintain a high level of spiritual awareness. This is the basic principle of happiness that I teach at my organization, Happy Science.

The second objective is to pursue public happiness. Thinking only about our own happiness or our spiritual well-being is not sufficient to create an ideal world on Earth. We must open our eyes and think about the happiness of those around us. The pursuit of public happiness is about contributing to the happiness of many people in society and in the world.

We should not leave this important mission to others. We need to look out at the world with excitement, learn, gain experience, offer suggestions for improvement, and take part in activities to make the world a better place. This is another basic principle of achieving happiness.

Each one of us has a responsibility to take action and be involved in activities to create an ideal world on Earth. It is not because of others, the government, or our circumstances that the world is not becoming a better place. It's the efforts that each one of us makes that will improve the world we live in.

We must not be content with achieving personal happiness. We can create an ideal world when our personal happiness and public happiness go hand in hand, together in harmony. The creation of an ideal world on Earth is the ultimate goal of Happy Science, and it is my earnest wish that many people will join our movement to achieve this goal.

AFTERWORD

This book is a collection of my ideas on the theme of progress, which is the fourth principle of the principles of happiness that I've developed. Also called the Fourfold Path, the Principles of Happiness consist of the principles of love, wisdom, self-reflection, and progress. By elevating the principle of progress from the personal to the national level, this book shows possibilities for the further development of my teachings on progress.

Chapter 5 addresses issues concerning politics on a national level. But specific issues such as whether the number of government workers and the current tax rates are appropriate deserve further consideration.

Ryuho Okawa

FOUNDER AND CEO
Happy Science Group

The contents of the following articles were compiled from the following sources authored by Ryuho Okawa:

Chapter 1: Becoming a Light of Happiness

"The Mindset for Triumphing in Life"
From *Invincible Thinking*, part 4 ("The Power of Invincible Thinking"), section 3 ("Transform Difficulties into Strength for Your Soul").

Chapter 4: Creating Your Own Destiny

"Authoring Our Own Life Story"
From *Shinri Bunmei No Ruten*, chapter 2 ("Kokoro No Kaitaku"), section 3 ("Unmei To Jiriki").

"Joan of Arc, a Girl Who Saved Her Country"
From *The Laws of Perseverance*, chapter 5 ("The Reversal of Your Common Sense"), section 1 ("The Battle Against the Common Sense of the Times").

"Life in this World Is Like a Movie"
From *The Challenge of Enlightenment*, chapter 5 ("Emptiness and Causality"), section 3 ("Emptiness (1): Transmigration between this World and the Spirit World").

"The Multidimensional Structure of the Spirit World"
From *Spiritual World 101*, part 1 ("There Is Nothing to Fear in Death Once You Know about the Other World"), chapter 2 ("Let's Learn about the Real State of Heaven and Hell").

"Japan, the Nation with the Longest History Under a Single Dynasty"
From *Nihon Kenkoku No Genten*, chapter 3 ("Nihon Kenkoku No Genten"), section 3 ("Nihon Bunmei No Roots Wo Saguru").

"The Fundamental Basis of Politics"
From *Nihon Kenkoku No Genten*, chapter 2 ("Seiji No Kongen Ni Arumono") section 4 ("Kami Ga Ningen Ni Takusareta Seiji No Risou Towa").

ABOUT THE AUTHOR

RYUHO OKAWA is Global Visionary, a renowned spiritual leader, and intrnational best-selling author with a simple goal: to help people find true happiness and create a better world.

His deep compassion and sense of responsibility for the happiness of each individual has prompted him to publish over 2,100 titles of religious, spiritual, and self-development teachings, covering a broad range of topics including how our thoughts influence reality, the nature of love, and the path to enlightenment. He also writes on the topics of management and economy, as well as the relationship between religion and politics in the global context. To date, Okawa's books have sold over 100 million copies worldwide and been translated into 28 languages.

Okawa has dedicated himself to improving society and creating a better world. In 1986, Okawa founded Happy Science as a spiritual movement dedicated to bringing greater happiness to humankind by uniting religions and cultures to live in harmony. Happy Science has grown rapidly from its beginnings in Japan to a worldwide organization with over twelve million members. Okawa is compassionately committed to the spiritual growth of others. In addition to writing and publishing books, he continues to give lectures around the world.

ABOUT HAPPY SCIENCE

Happy Science is a global movement that empowers individuals to find purpose and spiritual happiness and to share that happiness with their families, societies, and the world. With more than twelve million members around the world, Happy Science aims to increase awareness of spiritual truths and expand our capacity for love, compassion, and joy so that together we can create the kind of world we all wish to live in.

Activities at Happy Science are based on the Principles of Happiness (Love, Wisdom, Self-Reflection, and Progress). These principles embrace worldwide philosophies and beliefs, transcending boundaries of culture and religions.

Programs and Events

The doors of Happy Science are open to all. We offer a variety of programs and events, including self-exploration and self-growth programs, spiritual seminars, meditation and contemplation sessions, study groups, and book events.

For more information, visit happyscience-na.org or happy-science.org.

Contact Information

Happy Science is a worldwide organization with faith centers around the globe. For a comprehensive list of centers, visit the worldwide directory at happy-science. org or happyscience-na.org. The following are some of the many Happy Science locations:

United States and Canada

NEW YORK
79 Franklin Street New York, NY 10013 / Phone: 212-343-7972
Fax: 212-343-7973 / Email: ny@happy-science.org / Website: newyork.
happyscience-na.org

SAN FRANCISCO
525 Clinton Street Redwood City, CA 94062 / Phone&Fax: 650-363-2777 /
Email: sf@happy-science.org / Website: sanfrancisco.happyscience-na.org

FLORIDA
5208 8th St. Zephyrhills, FL 33542 / Phone: 813-715-0000 Fax: 813-715-0010 /
Email: florida@happy-science.org / Website: florida.happyscience-na.org

NEW JERSEY
725 River Rd. #102B Edgewater, NJ 07020 / Phone: 201-313-0127 Fax: 201-
313-0120 / Email: nj@happy-science.org / Website: newjersey.happyscience-na.
org

ATLANTA
1874 Piedmont Ave. NE Suite 360-C Atlanta, GA 30324 / Phone: 404-892-
7770 / Email: atlanta@happy-science.org / Website: atlanta.happyscience-na.
org

LOS ANGELES
1590 E. Del Mar Blvd. Pasadena, CA 91106 / Phone: 626-395-7775
Fax: 626-395-7776 / Email: la@happy-science.org / Website: losangeles.
happyscience-na.org

ORANGE COUNTY
10231 Slater Ave. #204 Fountain Valley, CA 92708 / Phone: 714-745-1140 /
Email: oc@happy-science.org

SAN DIEGO
Email: sandiego@happy-science.org

HAWAII
1221 Kapiolani Blvd. Suite 920 Honolulu, HI 96814 / Phone: 808-591-
9772 Fax: 808-591-9776 / Email: hi@happy-science.org / Website: hawaii.
happyscience-na.org

KAUAI
4504 Kukui Street, Dragon Building Suite 21 Kapaa, HI 96746 / Phone: 808-
822-7007 Fax: 808-822-6007 / Email: kauai-hi@happy-science.org / Website:
kauai.happyscience-na.org

TORONTO
323 College Street, Toronto, ON M5T 1S2 Canada / Phone&Fax: 1-416-
901-3747 / Email: toronto@happy-science.org / Website: happy-science.ca

VANCOUVER
#212-2609 East 49th Avenue, Vancouver, BC, V5S 1J9 Canada / Phone:
1-604-437-7735 Fax: 1-604-437-7764 / Email: vancouver@happy-science.org
/ Website: happy-science.ca

International

TOKYO
1-6-7 Togoshi Shinagawa,Tokyo, 142-0041 Japan / Phone: 81-3-6384-5770
Fax: 81-3-6384-5776 / Email: tokyo@happy-science.org / Website: happy-
science.org

LONDON
3 Margaret Street, London,W1W 8RE United Kingdom / Phone: 44-20-
7323-9255 Fax: 44-20-7323-9344 / Email: eu@happy-science.org / Website:
happyscience-uk.org

SYDNEY
516 Pacific Hwy Lane Cove North, 2066 NSW Australia / Phone: 61-2-
9411-2877 Fax: 61-2-9411-2822 / Email: sydney@happy-science.org

BRAZIL HEADQUARTERS
Rua. Domingos de Morais 1154,Vila Mariana, Sao Paulo, CEP 04009-002
Brazil / Phone: 55-11-5088-3800 Fax: 55-11-5088-3806 / Email: sp@happy-
science.org / Website: cienciadafelicidade.com.br

JUNDIAI
Rua Congo, 447, Jd.Bonfiglioli, Jundiai, CEP 13207-340 / Phone: 55-11-
4587-5952 / Email: jundiai@happy-sciece.org

SEOUL
74, Sadang-ro 27-gil, Dongjak-gu, Seoul, Korea / Phone: 82-2-3478-8777
Fax: 82-2- 3478-9777 / Email: korea@happy-science.org / Website:
happyscience-korea.org

TAIPEI
No. 89, Lane 155, Dunhua N. Road Songshan District Taipei City 105
Taiwan / Phone: 886-2-2719-9377 Fax: 886-2-2719-5570 / Email: taiwan@
happy-science.org / Website: happyscience-tw.org

MALAYSIA
No 22A, Block2, Jalil Link, Jalan Jalil Jaya 2, Bukit Jalil 57000, Kuala Lumpur
Malaysia / Phone: 60-3-8998-7877 Fax: 60-3-8998-7977 / Email: Malaysia@
happy-science.org / Website: happyscience.org.my

NEPAL

Kathmandu Metropolitan City, Ward No. 15, Ring Road, Kimdol, Sitapaila, Kathmandu Nepal / Phone: 977-1-427-2931 / Email: nepal@happy-science.org

UGANDA

Plot 877 Rubaga Road, Kampala P.O. Box 34130 Kampala, Uganda / Phone: 256-79-3238-002 / Email: uganda@happy-science.org / Website: happyscience-uganda.org

ABOUT IRH PRESS USA INC.

IRH Press USA Inc. was founded in 2013 as an affiliated firm of IRH Press Co., Ltd. Based in New York, the press publishes books in various categories including spirituality, religion, and self-improvement and publishes books by Ryuho Okawa, the author of 100 million books sold worldwide. For more information, visit OkawaBooks. com.

FOLLOW US ON:

FACEBOOK | MasterOkawaBooks

TWITTER | OkawaBooks

GOODREADS | RyuhoOkawa

INSTAGRAM | OkawaBooks

PINTEREST | OkawaBooks

BOOKS BY RYUHO OKAWA

THE HEART OF WORK
10 Keys to Living Your Calling

THINK BIG!
*Be Positive and Be Brave
to Achieve Your Dreams*

THE MIRACLE OF MEDITATION
*Opening Your Life to Peace,
Joy, and the Power Within*

THE ESSENCE OF BUDDHA
The Path to Enlightenment

THE LAWS OF JUSTICE
How We Can Solve World Conflicts and Bring Peace

MESSAGES FROM HEAVEN
*What Jesus, Buddha, Muhammad,
and Moses Would Say Today*

THE LAWS OF THE SUN
One Source, One Planet, One People

THE NINE DIMENSIONS
Unveiling the Laws of Eternity

For a complete list of books, visit OkawaBooks.com.